ANGELS

ANGELS: A HISTORICAL AND PROPHETIC STUDY

Printed in the United States of America

Published by
Hearthstone Publishing, Ltd.
500 Beacon Dr. ▪ Oklahoma City, OK 73127
405/789-3885 ▪ 800/652-1144 ▪ FAX 405/789-6502

Cover design by Christi Killian
ISBN 1-57558-030-6

ANGELS

A HISTORICAL & PROPHETIC STUDY

DR. BOB GLAZE

Acknowledgements

The author would like to thank the following for their help and encouragement in writing this book:

First and foremost I would like to thank my Lord and Savior Jesus Christ for His strength and guidance in my life as a Christian. His love is my inspiration and I can take no credit for this work. He has been my faithful Friend for over forty-seven years. His leading has always been toward my Father in heaven. And the Holy Spirit has always been my faithful helper and companion.

Second, I would like to express my love and appreciation for my wife of thirty-eight years, Peggy. She too has been a faithful, loving companion and friend through many years of toil and ministry. Also, for the many, many hours she has waited alone while I attended to the ministry, of which this book is only a small part. Never once has she questioned the Lord's leadership for our lives. Never once has she complained when I announced that the Lord was leading us in a different direction and it required a move to another city or even another state—she lives in expectancy, both now and toward eternity. Proverbs 12:4 sums it up best: "A virtuous woman is a crown to her husband."

Third, I would like to thank my uncle, Dr. Noah Hutchings, for the opportunity to minister at Southwest Radio Church. This ministry has opened up many new avenues of service. His knowledge and wit have been a constant encouragement and inspiration. His understanding and skill communicating the Word are truly amazing. It is an honor to serve by his side.

Also, I would like to thank the many others who had a part in this work. Ron King for the many hours spent in proofing the original text. Christi Killian for proofing, typesetting, and designing the cover. Also, for Janice Cheek and the many other staff members who covered for me as I worked on the manuscript. A special thanks to Marvin McElvany for the many times he rescued me from my computer and got me up and running one more time.

Table of Contents

Foreword

The Sadducees of Israel denied the existence of angels, and even today it is difficult to find an objective study on these spirit beings that presents factual, biblical information. So many who write on this subject tell the reader what they want to believe rather than the factual record of Scripture.

In this book Dr. Bob Glaze has covered the entire biblical scope of the activity and ministry of angels from Genesis to Revelation. The author also provides insight and scriptural light on angelic subjects for which Christians seek information:

- When were angels created?
- Why did God place cherubim at the Garden of Eden?
- Were the sons of God of Genesis 6 fallen angels?
- Are demons fallen angels?
- Who are the angels of Satan?
- Are all angels alike?
- Why the different orders of angels?
- Why did angelic activity increase during the years Jesus Christ was on earth?
- Do all angels have names?

- Why did angelic activity decline after Acts 13?
- What is the mission of angels in the Church age?
- Does every Christian have a guardian angel?
- Why will angelic activity increase in the Tribulation as indicated in Revelation?
- What will be the mission of angels during the Millennium?
- What will happen to the fallen angels?

We are indebted to Dr. Glaze for this refreshing book on the study of angels that lifts some of the doctrinal fog that has covered this subject for many years.

—Dr. Noah W. Hutchings, President
Southwest Radio Church

Introduction

If we believe that the Bible is the inspired, inerrant Word of God, then we also must believe in the literal existence of angels. We are informed in Scripture that angels were created by God as free moral agents. These beings had the choice to obey or disobey God. If they chose to disobey, it was at the beckoning of Satan from which they cannot repent. It is also indicated in Scripture that one-third of the angels chose to disobey, and they now follow Satan.

The Kingdom of God is indeed a kingdom, with angels divided into many different orders: watchers, holy ones, warrior angels, archangels, etc. In opposition to God and His angels are Satan and his angels. The ambition of Satan has never changed—to exalt his throne above the stars of God. This struggle, this war, will not be concluded until Satan and his angels are forever cast out of the heavens, defeated, and cast into the lake of fire and brimstone.

Angels have been mentioned in the Bible from Abraham ("by the oaks of Mamre") to John on the isle of Patmos. According to the *Pictorial Encyclopedia of the Bible,* "the earliest archaeological evidence of angels to date appears on the stele of Ur-Nammus, c. 2250 B.C., where angels are seen flying over the head of this king while in prayer." Angels are also a part of many different religions. For instance, the belief of angels is an essential part of Islam and necessary to becoming a Moslem. Angels are spirit beings, but can materialize with the appearance of men upon either their will or at the will or command of the Lord. According to Scripture, they were present when the earth was created. They were present in the Garden of Eden and witnessed the original sin of Adam and Eve and were placed at the garden entrance to guard the tree of life.

The "sons of God" who married the "daughters of men" referred to in the sixth chapter of Genesis were the angels that left their first estate, took upon themselves the form of men, and cohabited with women. After the flood, angels were sent on special assignments as God's messengers to fulfill His will—Sodom and Gomorrah is one of many examples.

Angels were very evident during the earthly ministry of Jesus because He was offering the kingdom of heaven to Israel at that time. However, after the thirteenth chapter of Acts when the offer of the kingdom to Israel was set aside and the Apostle Paul was sent to the Gentiles with the gospel of grace, the ministry of holy angels became less evident.

In this dispensation when God is calling out of the Gentiles a people to complete His church, Christians are to follow the leading of the indwelling Holy Spirit, not angels. The Apostle John wrote his gospel, according to chronologists, in A.D. 90, and he mentioned angels only four times in casual references, and not once in his three epistles. Yet in the Revelation John made sixty-eight references to angels. Why? Because in the Revelation the church in chapter four has been translated, and the indwelling ministry of the Holy Spirit has been removed from the world with the Church. With the absence of the Church, angelic activity will increase. The world is now being conditioned to the increased activity of angels in anticipation of the impending Tribulation period. During the Tribulation, the kingdom of God is imminent, and angels busily carry out the judgment determined to reclaim this planet and establish the Lord God as King of kings upon the throne of David.

Today, dozens of books are being written about angels. Television programs and movies are being mass produced which present angels as deceased humans, both male and female, that are trying to gain their wings by doing good deeds here on earth. It is being taught that each one of us has a guardian angel, especially children. It is being taught even though one and one-half million Jewish children died in the Holocaust and thousands of children are being killed or sexually molested each day. This does not mean that angels do not or cannot intervene in certain people's lives today, but according to Scripture this is by special assignment and not by divine entitlement. The undue stress today on the importance of angelic influence in the lives of Christians practically amounts to the worship of angels, which is strictly forbidden by God (Col. 2:18; Rev. 22:8–9).

The Christian's conception of biblical angels is distorted by the influence of the world's imagination. For instance, many Christians, along with most of the world, picture all angels having wings. While some angels are described as having wings, most are not described as winged creatures. The seraphim described in Isaiah 6:1–2 and Revelation 4:7–8 have wings. In Ezekiel 1:5–6 another winged angel is described, the cherubim. While it is possible that all angels in the Bible have wings, there is no scriptural proof. The lack of mention of wings in many important passages would suggest that most angels do not in fact have wings.

In recent testimonies it has been reported that certain individuals have been visited by angels. One of these reports suggested that on several occasions an unidentified angel would wake him at night and relate a prophetic message. The individual said that he was always at ease and never felt any anxiety or fear. These messages, however, were not divulged until after the prophesied events took place. Of course, his reluctance to come forth prior to the events and give the angel's message caused a serious credibility problem. His ease in the presence of the angel also added to his unbelievable story. In most instances the appearance of angels in Scripture is announced by the words, "fear not."

It is our prayer that this humble effort on the study of angels will at least provide the reader with a correct dispensational overview of the ministry of angels as presented in Scripture from Genesis to Revelation.

Chapter One

The Existence of Angels

The word "angel," or a form of the word "angel," is mentioned almost three hundred times in Scripture in some thirty-four books of both the Old and New Testament. Whether the word appears in the Hebrew form of the Old Testament, *malakh,* or the Greek form of the New Testament, *anggelos,* it simply means "messenger." The word in itself is nondescriptive and does not define any attributes, physical or moral, and only appears in the masculine gender. The writers of the Bible never try to prove their existence; they simply accept their existence as fact based upon their understanding of Scripture, the leadership of the Holy Spirit, and their own experience. Therefore, we must not depend on assumptions that angels exist, but upon the weight of revelation in Scripture.

To deny the existence of angels would be equal to denying the very Word of God. The portions of Scripture that contain narratives concerning angels are as much a part of God's Word as the story of creation, the Ten Commandments, the gospel accounts of the birth of Jesus, or the gospel of salvation. Although there are many personalities of angels in the Bible, there are two main distinctions: the angel of the Lord, and the generic term for messenger, angel. In this chapter we will concern ourselves with the existence of these two distinctions.

The Angel of the Lord

The first time we see the word "angel" appear in the Bible is in Genesis 16:7: "And the **angel** of the LORD found her by a fountain of water in the wilderness, by the fountain in the way to Shur." This passage concerns Sarah's maid Hagar who fled because of Sarah's harsh treatment. This is not the generic term for angel—it is *the angel of the Lord,* which is also synonymous with *the angel of Jehovah.* However, this person *is* referred to as an angel. Hagar recognized this person as more than mere mortal or even a messenger of God; she recognized him as God. How? Because he told her things that no man could know. She attests to this in verse 13: "And she called the name of the LORD that spake unto her, Thou God seest me: for she said, Have I also here looked after him that seeth me?" She had not only seen an angel, but also God. Charles Ryrie states in the *Ryrie Study Bible* that this is "a theophany, a self-manifestation of God. He here speaks as God, identifies Himself with God, and claims to exercise the prerogatives of God."

Lewis Sperry Chafer, in his *Systematic Theology,* quotes Walvoord's analysis of the angel of the Lord (Jehovah) as proof for the pre-existence of Christ. Walvoord states:

> A theophany is a manifestation of God in visible and bodily form before the incarnation. Usually the term

> *theophany* is limited to appearances of God in the form of man or angels, other phenomena such as the Shekinah glory not being considered a theophany. The theophanies are chiefly appearances of the Angel of Jehovah, who is clearly distinct from angelic beings.

While writing this account of the "angel of the Lord" in Genesis, Moses never questioned the fact that this truly happened. He saw no need to try to prove that it happened, based upon his own experience, for he too had encountered the angel of the Lord in "a flame of fire out of the midst of a bush" in Exodus 3. At this occasion, Moses was visibly drawn to a miraculous phenomenon in the form of a burning bush that was not consumed. Upon his arrival to the place of the burning bush, God called to him. We see no indication in Scripture that Moses had ever experienced anything similar to this, yet without hesitation he accepted the voice as that of the Lord. Also without hesitation, Moses answered God's call and challenge and spent the rest of his life in His service based upon his belief that this angel was truly the angel of the Lord.

The "angel of God" referred to in Exodus 14:19 can be no other than the same "angel of the Lord" seen in other passages. In verse 14 Moses told the complaining Israelites, "The LORD shall fight for you, and ye shall hold your peace." Then in verse 19 Moses writes: "And the angel of God, which went before the camp of Israel, removed and went behind them; and the pillar of the cloud went from before their face, and stood behind them."

This again is a theophany, or a physical manifestation of the Son of God.

Another theophany is found in Exodus 23:20–21:

> Behold, I send an Angel before thee, to keep thee in the way, and to bring thee into the place which I have prepared. Beware of him, and obey his voice, provoke him not; for he will not pardon your transgressions: for my name is in him.

This angel had the power to require the death penalty based upon His own judgments. He would also accompany them on their journey and judge their conduct. He also says that "my name is in him." In other words, they have the same name.

Perhaps the most unusual appearance of the angel of the Lord appears in Numbers chapter twenty-two. In this narrative, Moses and the children of Israel are advancing against those who possess the Promised Land. Moses and the children of Israel are camped on the bank of the Jordon River near Jericho, poised to continue their advancement against the Moabites. Balak, the king of Moab, is very afraid of Moses and his army and sends for a soothsayer named Balaam to curse Israel. Before Balaam was able to appear before Balak, the Lord interceded and instructed him on what he was to do and say. However, Balaam did not do as he was instructed and proceeded on his way to see Balak, no doubt with the thought of the promised fortune guiding his every step.

Here a most unusual thing happened. The angel of the Lord manifested Himself to Balaam's beast but remained invisible to Balaam. In Numbers 22:22–25 we continue Moses narration:

> And God's anger was kindled because he went: and the angel of the LORD stood in the way for an adversary against him. Now he was riding upon his ass, and his two servants were with him. And the ass saw the angel of the LORD standing in the way, and his sword drawn in his hand: and the ass turned aside out of the way, and went into the field: and Balaam smote the ass, to turn her into the way. But the angel of the LORD stood in a path of the vineyards, a wall being on this side, and a wall on that side. And when the ass saw the angel of the LORD, she thrust herself unto the wall, and crushed Balaam's foot against the wall: and he smote her again.

One remarkable thing here is not the fact that the beast saw what she considered a threat, but that she saw the angel of the Lord at all.

But the most remarkable thing in this text is the fact that the Lord gave the beast the ability to speak in verse 28: "And the LORD opened the mouth of the ass, and she said unto Baalam, What have I done unto thee, that thou hast smitten me these three times?" We find it uncanny that Balaam was not alarmed at the speech of his beast. He began to argue and carry on a conversation with her. Could it be that Balaam, being a soothsayer and representative of Satan, was familiar with this activity? Even the poor beast knew that you bow before the Creator of the universe, and fell to his knees. Then Balaam was forced to confess his sin and obey the angel of the Lord.

The lesson here is that the angel of the Lord was God,

who can loose the tongue of a dumb beast, and can also bind the tongue of the talking beast, proving that He was indeed God. Finally, as Willmington points out, the outcome of Balaam's confrontation with the one who hired him, Balak and Moab, received the curse meant for Israel in the form of a prophecy. "Balaam's final words about Israel (24:10–25) included references to a 'star' and 'scepter'—prophecies ultimately fulfilled by the Messiah" (*Willmington's Guide to the Bible,* p. 86) —represented here by the angel of the Lord.

The angel of the Lord was active throughout the Old Testament and championed many as well as destroyed many. He was always faithful to those who were faithful to Him. In Judges 6 the angel of the Lord stood with Gideon and conquered the Midianites. In Judges 14, the angel of the Lord was the strength of Samson as he overcame the Philistines. In 2 Samuel 24, the angel of the Lord stood by David and stayed the hand of the angel sent to destroy Jerusalem. Paul states in 2 Corinthians 13:1, "In the mouth of two or three witnesses shall every word be established." In Malachi 4:4–5 the two witnesses God has established are the Law and the prophets. If there were no other witnesses they would certainly be sufficient. Malachi states:

> Remember ye the law of Moses my servant, which I commanded unto him in Horeb for all Israel, with the statutes and judgments. Behold, I will send you Elijah the prophet before the coming of the great and dreadful day of the LORD.

The Law and the prophets are the two witnesses, and

Moses and Elijah are their representatives. We have already looked at Moses. Now let us look to Elijah.

The angel of the Lord was very active in the life and ministry of Elijah, who was empowered by Him on many occasions. The first occasion the angel was mentioned is in 1 Kings 19:5, and the second time in 19:7. Here the angel of the Lord prepared bread and water to sustain Elijah for forty days on his journey to mount Horeb. His miracles included his declaration of a long drought (1 Kings 17:1); multiplying the widow's flour and oil (1 Kings 17: 7–16); the resurrection of the widow's son (1 Kings 17:17–24); calling down fire from heaven (1 Kings 18:1–40); sending a rainstorm (1 Kings 18:41–45); outrunning a chariot (1 Kings 18:46); predicting Ahaziah's death (2 Kings 1:1–17); calling down fire from heaven to kill Ahaziah's men (2 Kings 1:9–17); and parting the Jordan (2 Kings 2:1–8).

The last time we see the angel of the Lord with Elijah is in 2 Kings 1:15. Here Elijah was encouraged by the Lord to tell Ahaziah that he would never arise from his deathbed. Soon after this, Elijah was escorted from this earth in a whirlwind without seeing death, being whisked away by the angel of the Lord, the God he had served all of his ministry.

In Daniel we see the pre-incarnate Christ in the form of the angel of the Lord in 3:24–25, the narrative of the vindication of the three Hebrew children. They had refused to obey the king and said simply in verses 17–18:

> If it be so, our God whom we serve is able to deliver us from the burning fiery furnace, and he will deliver

> us out of thine hand, O king. But if not, be it known unto thee, O king, that we will not serve thy gods, nor worship the golden image which thou hast set up.

The Lord appeared in verses 24 and 25:

> Did not we cast three men bound into the midst of the fire? They answered and said unto the king, True, O king. He answered and said, Lo, I see four men loose, walking in the midst of the fire, and they have no hurt; and the form of the fourth is like the Son of God.

Truly this is the "angel of the Lord," and was recognized as such by the king himself by some supernatural means. This is the same angel that saved Daniel from the lions' den in chapter six. In verse 22 Daniel gives the king the good news that the angel had stayed the night with him. "My God hath sent his angel, and hath shut the lions' mouths, that they have not hurt me." This was the same angel that came to the rescue of the three Hebrews in the fiery furnace.

The angel of the Lord in the Old Testament was truly the pre-incarnate Christ. Here we can study the Son of God historically. In John 1:1 we read that before there was even time, Christ who created everything was already in existence. He was active and committed to preserving His creation and providing a way for man to ultimately have communion again with Him. This He did as the distinct personality of the angel of the Lord. He was everywhere and always present in the affairs of man and had definite and repeated dealings with the Israelites.

Although He speaks as God, identifies Himself with God, and claims to exercise the prerogatives of God, He distinguishes Himself from Yahweh. "That He is a member of the Trinity is indicated by the fact that the appearances of the Angel of Yahweh cease after the incarnation" (Charles Ryrie, *Basic Theology,* p. 239). Paul attests to His Old Testament presence in the New Testament book of 1 Corinthians 10:1–4:

> Moreover, brethren, I would not that ye should be ignorant, how that all our fathers were under the cloud, and all passed through the sea; And were all baptized unto Moses in the cloud and in the sea; And did all eat the same spiritual meat; And did all drink the same spiritual drink: for they drank of that spiritual Rock that followed them: and that Rock was Christ.

The scriptural proof that the angel of the Lord was Christ incarnate in the Old Testament is overwhelming, but perhaps one of the greatest proofs is that the angel of the Lord no longer appears after the birth of Christ. In all the appearances of angels in the New Testament, the angel of the Lord does not appear. The Old Testament reveals the angel of Jehovah as sent by Jehovah to reveal truth, to lead Israel, and to defend and judge them.

In the New Testament, Christ is sent by God to reveal God in the flesh, to reveal truth, and to become the Savior. In the nature of the Trinity it is the Father who sends the Son and the Spirit, the First Person never having sent Himself. The similar character of ministry of the angel of Jehovah and Christ would serve to identify them. By process of elimination it can be demonstrated that the angel of Jehovah must be the Second Person. According to John 1:18, "No man hath seen God at any time; the only begotten Son, which is in the bosom of the Father, he hath declared him."

The theophanies of the Old Testament, being the manifestation of Christ, the Second Person in visible form, constitute an argument for the pre-existence in history, as contrasted to the direct statement of the New Testament. Therefore, the identity of the angel of the Lord passes from a theophany in the Old Testament to that of the man Christ Jesus in the New Testament.

Angels as Messengers

The second type of angels mentioned in the Bible is the generic term angels or messengers. The proof of their existence is stated in Scripture by the overwhelming number of times they are noted. Nowhere in the Bible is their existence questioned. In every case the writers of the Bible assume their existence without hesitation. They are spirit beings created by our Lord, as stated in Colossians 1:16–17:

> For by him were all things created, that are in heaven, and that are in earth, visible and invisible, whether they be thrones, or dominions, or principalities, or powers: all things were created by him, and for him: And he is before all things, and by him all things consist.

We must also assume from these verses that all angels were created at the same time. We see no place in Scripture that their number was ever added to or subtracted from the original number. Of this Chafer states:

> In like manner, it is assumed that the creation of angels was completed at that time and that none will be added to their number. They are not subject to death or any form of extinction, therefore they do not decrease as they do not increase. The plan by which the human family is secured through propagation has no counterpart among the angels. Each angel, being a direct creation of God, stands in immediate and personal relation to the Creator. Of certain of the human family as they appear in the next world, it is said by Christ, "They neither marry, nor are given in marriage, but are as the angels of God in heaven" (Matt. 22:28–30).
>
> —Lewis Sperry Chafer,
> *Systematic Theology, Vol. 2,* p. 11

Thus it is concluded as that there is no decrease or increase among the heavenly beings.

The Bible has much to say about multitudes of angels, but we are not told the exact number. Some idea is given in Revelation 5:11 where it says: "And I beheld, and I heard the voice of many angels round about the throne and the beasts and the elders: and the number of them was ten thousand times ten thousand, and thousands of thousands."

That can be understood as millions. Also, Matthew

26:53 reports Christ said that He could call down thirty-six to seventy-two thousand angels.

So, we know that there are many, many angels; they are innumerable. Daniel 7:10 mentions that there are millions of angels: ". . . thousand thousands ministered unto him, and ten thousand times ten thousand stood before him." The number of angels is not known—perhaps as many as the grains of sand on the shore.

In Revelation 12 we are told that one-third of the angels, however many that was, followed Lucifer. This means that one-third of the angels are fallen angels. These fallen angels along with holy angels are active today. Many Christians and non-Christians alike claim to have seen angels. Some individuals believe they have guardian angels. How do we know that there are such things as spirit beings? Can we dismiss their existence because they cannot be seen?

Suppose someone walking by a lake had never seen a fish and knew nothing about them. Although there is no evidence of fish, because they are all beneath the surface, he sees a ripple and wonders what is causing it. Equally, even though we may not see an angel in this life, we know they exist by their activity.

Consider that until about one hundred and twenty-five years ago no one knew that there was a world of minute organisms, germs, and viruses. If you had told someone then that they were surrounded by millions of microbes, germs, and viruses which were causing some of the illnesses of the day, you would not have been believed. Just because we cannot see angels, or have not seen angels, does not mean that they do not exist. Nor does it mean that every unexplainable or unusual happening can be attributed to them. Again, however, we know they exist and are active because Scripture tells us that they exist and are active.

> In our day neoorthodoxy's (sic) denial of the objective existence of angels has been countered by the widespread publicity given to demons and their activity. While people may deny theologically the existence of an order of beings called angels (and demons), practically their reported activity seems to make it impossible to deny their existence. Thus on the one hand man's bias against anything supernatural rules out in his mind the existence of angels; while on the other hand activity which he cannot explain rationally makes their existence seem necessary.
>
> —Charles Ryrie, *Basic Theology,* p. 121

It seems, therefore, that man does not have the natural ability or insight to explain away the possibility that angels do exist, or the ability to explain away the possibility that they do not exist. Today, people are being conditioned to accept unexplainable events as the activity of angels. We are being psychologically honed with conditioned response. This activity as pointed out in Scripture will increase greatly as we approach the impending Tribulation. All possible occurrences of angelic activity must be interpreted in light of Scripture, and there are many examples in the Bible to guide our interpretation.

In *Basic Theology,* Ryrie states that "if one accepts the biblical revelation then there can be no question about the existence of angels." He goes on to add three significant characteristics about the revelation of angels. First, the mention of angels appears over one hundred times in the Old Testament and about one hundred and sixty-five times in the New Testament. He also points out that it only takes one mention in Scripture to establish its truth. Second, angels are mentioned throughout the Bible and are not confined to one period of history or to one writer. Third, the Lord refers to angels a number of times. To then deny their existence would cast doubt on His veracity.

Angels were created to worship and praise their Creator by attending to His creation. Their worship involves delivering the will of God by word and by deed. They exist to serve. To try to determine why the Lord chose or even needed these messengers is equal in determining the reason Christ had to die to save mankind. By faith we accept our Lord as our Savior without ever seeing Him physically. Our eternal destiny is determined by faith, not sight. We know He lives because His witness is embedded within our very spirits. We see the evidence of His existence in the events of our lives and the state of the world. His Spirit bears witness with our spirit. We believe based upon His eternal Word.

It should not be unreasonable to accept the existence of angels. Paul states: "So then faith cometh by hearing, and hearing by the word of God" (Rom. 10:17). The Word of God states that angels exist, therefore, angels exist. The belief and acceptance of the existence of angels is necessary to carry on the remainder of the study of angels. We now need to examine their creation and nature.

Chapter Two

The Creation and Nature of Angels

The Time of Creation of Angels

The purpose of angels is to worship and praise the Creator. This is the reason they were created. One of their duties was to attend to God's creation as they were instructed. This came in the form of delivering messages and at times intervening in the affairs of man. It was therefore necessary that they were created prior to the things that they were to attend. We could compare this to the question: Which came first, the chicken or the egg? Certainly, we know that the chicken was created first, not the egg. It takes a rooster to make the egg fertile, without which it would not produce a baby chick. All of creation was created with maturity.

When living on the farm as a boy, even I knew that eggs would not hatch out on their own. Something, a hen in this case, had to sit on the egg to incubate it. Left unattended, the eggs would spoil. In the same way it was therefore necessary for the angels to be created prior to the creation they were to attend.

In the story of the creation in Genesis, we see no mention of the creation of angels. The creation of every other thing was mentioned and explained in order of their creation, except the angels. Therefore, when were they created? The only scriptural evidence we find is in the narrative of Job 38. In verses 4–7, we read:

> Where wast thou when I laid the foundations of the earth? declare, if thou hast understanding. Who hath laid the measures thereof, if thou knowest? or who hath stretched the line upon it? Whereupon are the foundations thereof fastened? or who laid the corner stone thereof; When the morning stars sang together, and all the sons of God shouted for joy?

Here God is reminding Job that he is ignorant compared to his Creator. Job, if you are so smart, then how and when was the earth created?

The only witnesses other than the Creator were the "morning stars and the sons of God." The question is, who are "the morning stars and the sons of God"? If they are angels, then we have evidence as to the time of their creation. Most writers agree that they are indeed the angels.

In Job 1:6, we read: "Now there was a day when the sons of God came to present themselves before the Lord, and Satan came also among them." Here we see a group of created beings reporting to the Lord. It could only be angels because Satan is among them, and we know from Scripture that he is certainly an angel. In *The Apocalypse* Seiss states that these are most certainly angels, but makes no distinction between the morning stars and the sons of God. The scene we are considering is the time when the earth was created. Man was not present, only God, the morning stars, and the sons of God.

The morning stars could not have been the physical lights we see by night, because they were not created until the fourth day. "And God made two great lights; the greater light to rule the day, and the lesser light to rule the night: he made the stars also. . . . And the evening and the morning were the fourth day" (Gen. 1:16,19).

The sons of God could not have been the godly line of Seth or man in general, because man was not created until the sixth day.

> So God created man in his own image, in the image of God created he him; male and female created he them. . . . And God saw every thing that he had made, and, behold, it was very good. And the evening and the morning were the sixth day
>
> —Genesis 1:27, 31

We must agree that all physical creation was created within six twenty-four hour days. However, it appears that all spirit beings were created prior to the physical creation. The one possible exception is that of the soul and spirit of man, but we will not examine that in this work.

The Nature of Angels

In attempting to investigate the nature of angels we must determine several things. We must first know the makeup of their being. We must also know about their non-moral attributes such as omnipotence, omniscience, omnipresence, and immutability. These are the attributes of God, but do the angels possess them? Are they eternal or temporal? What is their gender and can they procreate? To whom are they subordinate? These questions we must address in order to discover the nature of these beings.

We have previously examined the time of angels creation, but what is their makeup? Do they have flesh and blood as humans, or were they created into another dimension visible only within a spiritual world? We find the answer to this in Hebrews 1:7: "And of the angels he saith, Who maketh his angels spirits, and his ministers a flame of fire." Here they are described as spirits, not having human bodies. We see there is a difference in the two in 1 Corinthians 15:44: ". . . There is a natural body, and there is a spiritual body." Here Chafer states of angels:

> Their natures do not include bodies unless they are bodies of a spiritual order (1 Cor. 15:44), although they may be seen at times in bodies and appear as men (Matt. 28:3: Rev. 15:6; 18:1). Thus, while they are similar to man in personality, they differ from man in many important particulars.
>
> —Lewis Sperry Chafer, *Major Bible Themes,* p. 152

Angels as spirit beings are immaterial and incorporeal. While we cannot under normal circumstances see angels, they evidently can see humans, because we are told that they are "ministering spirits" in Hebrews 1:14. It would seem logical that we could not be ministered unto unless we can be seen.

Angels are normally invisible unless the eyesight is augmented, as in the case of the young man in 2 Kings 6:15–17.

> And when the servant of the man of God was risen early, and gone forth, behold, an host compassed the city both with horses and chariots. And his servant said unto him, Alas, my master! how shall we do? And he answered, Fear not: for they that be with us are more than they that be with them. And Elisha prayed, and said, LORD, I pray thee, open his eyes, that he may see. And the LORD opened the eyes of the young man; and he saw: and, behold, the mountain was full of horses and chariots of fire round about Elisha.

This event may be played out millions of times each day, only we cannot see it. One reason is that if we could see angels, their awe would cause most to worship them.

Under the broad spectrum of angels is also included those with other names. Of this Ryrie states:

> Angels, demons (assuming they are fallen angels), and Satan belong to a class of beings which may be labeled spirit beings. Angels are said to be ministering spirits (Heb. 1:14). Demons are called evil and unclean spirits (Luke 8:2; 11:24, 26), and Satan is the spirit that now works in the sons of disobedience (Eph. 2:2).
>
> —Charles Ryrie, *Basic Theology,* p. 126

Therefore, regardless of the moral state of the angel, Satan is considered an angel.

The only times we see angels take on human-like appearance is by special assignment, and then we are not sure if the angels change their properties or those who see are given special sight. We need only one example to press the point. In Genesis 18:1–2, we read the beginning of the account between the Lord and Abraham of the coming destruction of Sodom and Gomorrah:

> And the LORD appeared unto him in the plains of Mamre: and he sat in the tent door in the heat of the day; And he lift up his eyes and looked, and, lo, three men stood by him: and when he saw them, he ran to meet them from the tent door, and bowed himself toward the ground.

Here the Lord, as well as the two angels, appeared to Abraham as men.

After the prophecy concerning the future son of Abraham and Sarah, the Lord turned His attention toward Sodom. We see in verse 22 that while the Lord stayed behind with Abraham, the two men went toward Sodom. When the Lord had completed His business, He went His way. However, we read in Genesis 19:1 that the two men are now called angels. "And there came two angels to Sodom at even." We have no scriptural reason to believe that they are two different beings from the ones that had been with Abraham earlier. Why were the angels there? To retrieve Lot and his family from the terrible sin of the city—homosexuality. The state of homosexuality in Sodom is common knowledge, and we will not dwell on that sin.

The point here is that in verse 10 the two angels displayed their physical properties by physically pulling Lot back inside his house. Here we have an instance of a special assignment, the spiritual becoming physical to accomplish a task that could not be done by a spirit being. The angels then "smote the men that were at the door of the house with blindness, both small and great" (vs. 11). The angels were acting under the enabling power of God. We see here not the miracle of sight but the miracle of blindness. This, along with many other texts, is proof that angels do at times take on physical properties which are not their natural state.

Non-moral attributes are those that are inherent, but are not concerned with good or evil. The first of these attributes to consider is omnipotence. Omnipotence is the attribute of being all-powerful; having no limitations. Certainly, we know that God is all-powerful, but did He create any of His angels with this attribute?

Angels are supernatural and superhuman in strength, but they are not all-powerful. "Whereas angels, which are greater in power and might, bring not railing accusation against them before the Lord" (2 Pet. 2:11). Here they are reticent to speak about humans, even evil humans. Why would spirit beings that are much more powerful than man restrain themselves from judging him? Perhaps we get the answer from Paul in 1 Cor. 6:2–3:

> Do ye not know that the saints shall judge the world? and if the world shall be judged by you, are ye unworthy to judge the smallest matters? Know ye not that we shall judge angels? how much more things that pertain to this life?

This would give us an indication that they hold themselves in restraint because of fear—not the fear of respect, but the fear of retribution.

They are certainly more powerful than man during this age, but in the future they will become less powerful than man. Here Ryrie states about them concerning 2 Peter 2:11:

> *against them.* Probably a reference to the false teachers. In other words, even though the false teachers speak evil of angels, angels do not denounce them but leave all judgment to God. Some interpret *them* to refer to evil angels; i.e., good angels do not accuse evil angels.
>
> —Charles Ryrie, *Ryrie Study Bible,* p. 1893

In either case, we can deduce that the angels are less that omnipotent.

The best indication that angels are not omnipotent is that the most powerful angel, Lucifer, is directly under the control of God. In Job chapter one we see that the sons of God, including Satan (the angel Lucifer) presented themselves to God. The angels were summoned to the presence of God to report on their activities. This alone proves that they are answerable to someone, which means that they are not omnipotent.

When Satan was questioned about his activity, he was asked if he had considered God's servant Job. His answer to God was that he had not considered him because he was off limits. God then told Satan that he could take all that Job had, but could not touch his body. In verse 12 we see Satan's limitations: "And the LORD said unto Satan, Behold, all that he hath is in thy power; only upon himself put not forth thine hand. So Satan went forth from the presence of the LORD." Satan did not argue with God; he left to carry out His instructions. His acceptance of these conditions is proof that he acknowledged that he was less powerful than God.

In Revelation 12:7–12 we read that Satan and his angels will be cast out of heaven. He, along with his angels, are less powerful than Christ and His angels. In Revelation 20:10 we see the final result of Satan's lack of omnipotence. "And the devil that deceived them was cast into the lake of fire and brimstone, where the beast and the false prophet are, and shall be tormented day and night for ever and ever." Seiss has this to say of Satan: "He was imprisoned in the Abyss before; but he is now 'cast in the lake of fire and brimstone, where also the Beast and the false Prophet [are]'" (*The Apocalypse,* p. 478).

When the Savior was on earth, he discoursed to His disciples about an "everlasting fire, prepared for the devil and his angels" (Matt. 25:41). That is it; and this is the time when he for whom it is prepared first feels those terrific flames. Hard as he tried, Satan could not overcome his subservient position under the omnipotent God.

Thiessen adds the following concerning the omnipotence of angels.

> They are said to be greater in might and power than man (2 Pet. 2:11; cf. "mighty in strength," Ps. 103:20). Paul calls them "mighty angels" (2 Thess. 1:7). Illus-

> trations of the power of angels are found in the freeing of the apostles from prison (Acts 5:19; 12:7) and the rolling away of the stone from the tomb (Matt. 28:2). They are limited in strength as seen in the warfare between the good and the evil angels (Rev. 12:7). The angel who came to Daniel needed assistance from Michael in his struggle with the prince of Persia (Dan. 10:13). Neither Michael the archangel (Jude 9) nor Satan (Job 1:12; 2:6) has unlimited power.
>
> —*Lectures in Systematic Theology,* p. 134

The lack of the omnipotence of angels is well documented in Scripture, as well as documenting their weaknesses.

The next non-moral attribute to examine is the omniscience of angels. Omniscience is the state of having infinite awareness, understanding, and insight, possessing universal or complete knowledge and unlimited in creative power.

Angels are stated to have great wisdom. "To fetch about this form of speech hath thy servant Joab done this thing: and my lord is wise, according to the wisdom of an angel of God, to know all things that are in the earth" (2 Sam. 14:20). These were words of flattery to impress Joab. His wisdom was being compared to the wisdom of *an* angel of God who knows everything about the earth, not *the* angel of God who is omniscient. To have great wisdom or knowledge is not equal to knowing all things. Even though angels do possess more knowledge than man, they do not know everything.

Another reason that we can know that angels are not omniscient is that they do not know the time of the Lord's return. In Matthew 24 the Lord is comparing the time of His return to Noah's day. Before the flood men did not receive Noah's message of impending judgment, and therefore were unprepared for the event. These same conditions will exist when the Lord returns: men ignoring the warnings and being unprepared.

We will know the season of His return because the conditions will be similar, but the exact time is a secret. In verse 36 we learn that even the angels don't know the time. "But of that day and hour knoweth no man, no, not the angels of heaven, but my Father only."

In Mark 13:32 the Son is added to the list of those who do not know the time of the return of the Lord. Some believe that this literally means to convey that the Son of God does not know the time of His return. Brown adds:

> This very remarkable statement regarding "the Son" is peculiar to Mark. Whether it means that the Son was not at that time in possession of the knowledge referred to, or simply that it was not among the things which He had received to communicate—has been matter of much controversy even amongst the firmest believers in the proper Divinity of Christ. . . . Beyond all doubt, as the word "knoweth" [*oiden*] in this verse is the well-known word for the knowledge of any fact, this latter sense is the one we should naturally put upon the statement; namely that our Lord did not at that time know the day and hour of His own Second Coming.
>
> —D. A. Brown, *Commentary, Vol. 3,* p. 195

This would seem untenable. As a man only, perhaps this

would be true. However, He is God-Man, therefore He would be omniscient. We see in Scripture that the Father, who is omniscient, knows the time of the Son's return; therefore the Son would know: "I and my Father are one" (John 10:30). In John 14:9 we see this once again stated: "Jesus saith unto him, Have I been so long time with you, and yet hast thou not known me, Philip? he that hath seen me hath seen the Father; and how sayest thou then, Shew us the Father?"

Therefore, it would only seem reasonable that the Son did in fact know the hour—not as man, but as God. To conclude that the Son knows no more than the angels would be tantamount to placing Him as only their equal. The angels do not know the hour because they are not omniscient.

Another narrative to prove that angels are not omniscient is 1 Peter 1:11–12:

> Searching what, or what manner of time the Spirit of Christ which was in them did signify, when it testified beforehand the sufferings of Christ, and the glory that should follow. Unto whom it was revealed, that not unto themselves, but unto us they did minister the things, which are now reported unto you by them that have preached the gospel unto you with the Holy Ghost sent down from heaven; which things the angels desire to look into.

Kenneth Wuest, in defining this passage states:

> Thus the angels peer into the mysteries of Church truth from beside it, like the cherubim bending over

> the Mercy Seat where man has access to God through a substitutionary sacrifice that cleanses him from sin. They are not participants in the salvation but spectators of it. Paul writing in a context of this mystery says, "To the intent that now unto the principalities and powers in heavenly places might be known by the church the manifold wisdom of God" (Eph. 3:10). The principalities and powers are of course the holy angels. The manifold wisdom of God as seen in the context is the truth of the Body of Christ. "Might be known" is passive and is more properly rendered "might be made known." "By" is the translation of *dia,* the preposition of intermediate agency. That is, this truth is to be made known to the holy angels by means of the instrumentality of the Church. The Church is the teacher of the angels. Paul says that the apostles "are made a spectacle unto the world, and to angels, and to men" (1 Cor. 4:9). How the angels watch the saints. How they wonder at creatures once totally depraved, now living lives that glorify God. It is in the Church that they catch the supreme view of God's love, sinners saved by grace, raised to a seat in the heavenly places in Christ. The Church is God's university foı angels.
>
> —*Word Studies in the Greek New Testament,*
> *Vol.* 2, p. 32

When the angels were created they were created holy, but not omniscient. They lived and worshipped under the command and law of God, but they could not understand the grace of God until their Creator died for the sins of man. Not knowing and understanding grace meant that they were not omniscient. Seeing that the angels were neither omnipotent nor omniscient, we now need to look at the attribute of omnipresence.

Omnipresence is having the ability to be everywhere present; being in more than one place at the same time. In order to test the omnipresence of angels they must be compared to the omnipresence of God Himself. Thiessen says this about the omnipresence of God:

> God is present in all his creation, but in no manner limited by it. Whereas immensity emphasized the transcendence of God in that he transcends all space and is not subject to the limitations of space, omnipresence has special reference to his presence within the universe (1 Kings 8:27; Ps. 139:7–10; Isa. 66:1; Jer. 23:23f.; Acts 7:48f.; 17:24f.; Rom. 10;6–8). It must be remembered that the omnipresence of God is not a necessary part of his being, but is a free act of his will. If God should will to destroy the universe, his omnipresence would cease, but he himself would not cease to be.
>
> —*Lectures in Systematic Theology*, p. 80

To this Shedd adds some good insight: "The Divine omnipresence means rather the presence of all things to God, than God's presence to all things. They are in his presence, but he is not in their presence."

When it is said in Jeremiah 23:24, "Do not I fill heaven and earth? saith the LORD," the language is tropical. If God were literally contained in the universe, the universe would be more immense than He is. In the first chapter of Romans, Paul discusses the creator-creature distinction. Here he states that, of necessity, the creator must be greater than his creation.

Certainly, we know that God is greater than His creation and is therefore omnipresent to creation. However, this relationship can only exist with God and His creation. Since the angels are created beings, they cannot contain or be omnipresent to creation. Angels are created beings and therefore can be only one place at a time. They, like all created beings, are localized. There are many Bible verses that prove this point, of which we will investigate only a few.

In Job 1 we see that the angels are summoned into the presence of God. They were already in the presence of God wherever they had been located. However, this was not for God's benefit, but for theirs. They were collectively summoned to one place that together they could witness the power and sovereignty of their Creator.

In Luke 8 we read a most unusual narrative concerning demons, or fallen angels. Here it is said that a man was possessed by many devils. "And Jesus asked him, saying, What is thy name? And he said, Legion: because many devils were entered into him" (vs. 30). Jesus had commanded the demons to come out of the man, and they begged Him not to cast them out into the deep. They asked, rather, to be cast into a herd of swine that were feeding nearby. Upon leaving the man, they entered the swine which promptly ran down the hill into the lake to a death of drowning rather than be possessed by the demons. The point is that the angels (demons) were bound or localized within the bodies of the swine and were not allowed freedom, proving that they were not omnipresent.

In discussing the sin of the angels of Genesis 6, Peter has this to say about their lack of omnipresence. Second Peter 2:4 states: "For if God spared not the angels that sinned, but cast them down to hell, and delivered them into chains of darkness, to be reserved unto judgment." It was not their omnipresence that was curtailed, but their freedom to roam. Omnipresence would eliminate the possibility of localizing and placing them in chains.

Finally, in Revelation 12:7–9, John tells of a war in heaven. Although Satan had lost his abode in heaven in the distant past, he still has the freedom to approach the throne of God in heaven to accuse the saints, much as he did in Job chapter one. Finally, in this narrative, Satan loses his freedom of access to the throne. He and his angels are cast down to the earth. We read:

> And there was war in heaven: Michael and his angels fought against the dragon; and the dragon fought and his angels, And prevailed not; neither was their place found any more in heaven. And the great dragon was cast out, that old serpent, called the Devil, and Satan, which deceiveth the whole world: he was cast out into the earth, and his angels were cast out with him.

In Revelation 20:1–3, we read:

> And I saw an angel come down from heaven, having the key of the bottomless pit and a great chain in his

> hand. And hc laid hold on the dragon, that old serpent, which is the Devil, and Satan, and bound him a thousand years, And cast him into the bottomless pit, and shut him up, and set a seal upon him, that he should deceive the nations no more, till the thousand years should be fulfilled: and after that he must be loosed a little season.

Again in verse 7: "And when the thousand years are expired, Satan shall be loosed out of his prison." Satan and his angels will be chained and imprisoned, or localized. They have lost their ability to roam freely, proving that angels are not everywhere present. The last non-moral attribute to examine is immutability.

Immutability is the act of never changing. We read in Hebrews 6:17–18 that God is immutable:

> Wherein God, willing more abundantly to shew unto the heirs of promise the immutability of his counsel, confirmed it by an oath: That by two immutable things, in which it was impossible for God to lie, we might have a strong consolation, who have fled for refuge to lay hold upon the hope set before us.

These immutable things are His word and His oath. This is the only place that the immutability is found in the Bible. No other person is said to be immutable other than God Himself. In James 1:17 God is spoken of as "the Father of lights, with whom is no variableness, neither shadow of turning." God does not cast a shadow or change the intensity of His light because He never changes or moves from His original position. He is the Giver of good gifts. He treats all men the same, without favor, as seen in Acts 10:34: ". . . that God is no respecter of persons."

His immutability is also seen in Hebrews 13:8: "Jesus Christ the same yesterday, and to-day, and for ever." God never changes, and angels must be compared to Him in judging their immutability.

If the position of angels has changed since their creation then we can safely say that they are not immutable.

> But there is every reason to believe that the angels were created perfect. In the creation account (Gen. 1), we are told seven times over that all that God made was good. In Gen. 1:31 we read, "And God saw all that He had made, and behold, it was very good." Surely that includes the perfection of the angels in holiness when originally created. If Ezek. 28:15 refers to Satan, as many suggest, then Satan is definitely said to have been created perfect. But various Scriptures represent some of the angels as evil (Ps. 78:49; Matt. 25:41; Rev. 9:11; 12:7–9). This is because they sinned, having left their own principality and proper abode (2 Pet. 2:4; Jude 6).
>
> —*Lectures in Systematic Theology,* p. 135

The change the angels experience was moral as well as positional. They became evil and also lost their original estate before God.

The angels' position also changed in reference and comparison to man. In Hebrews 2:7 man is said to have been created below the majesty of the angels. "Thou madest him a little lower than the angels; thou crownedst him with glory and honour, and didst set him over the works of thy hands." Although the angels were created above man, Paul states in 1 Corinthians 6:3 that this position will change in the future. "Know ye not that we shall judge angels?" It makes little or no difference if the position of the angels is lowered or the position of man is elevated, there is a change in the angels' power. This alone proves that the angels are not immutable.

We have seen that angels were created prior to the creation of the physical universe. They were created perfect as a spirit being. They do not possess a physical body apart from special manifestations ordered by God. They do not possess the non-moral attributes of God. They are not all-powerful, all-knowing, everywhere present, and do not possess the ability to remain unchanged. The nature of angels is ordered and controlled by their Creator, God Himself.

Chapter Three

The State of Angels

The state of the angels falls into two categories, holy and unholy. While we have already established that all angels were created perfect at their creation, we also see that some have fallen, or sinned. These angels that have sinned are called fallen angels, or demons. We see in Scripture that there are fallen angels that are free, and fallen angels that are in prison. There are many different types of angels that fall into the general classification of angels, but we will concern ourselves with only holy or unholy angels in this chapter. We will first investigate the holy angels.

The Holy Angels

> Praise ye the LORD. Praise ye the LORD from the heavens: praise him in the heights. Praise ye him, all his angels: praise ye him, all his hosts. Praise ye him, sun and moon: praise him, all ye stars of light. Praise him, ye heavens of heavens, and ye waters that be above the heavens. Let them praise the name of the LORD: for he commanded, and they were created.
>
> —Psalm 148:1–5

God created the angels the same way He created the physical universe: He spoke them into existence. He who creates can also destroy. The physical He will destroy, and the spiritual He will preserve. Angels are spirit beings, and holy or unholy they will never die. "Neither can they die any more: for they are equal unto the angels; and are the children of God, being the children of the resurrection" (Luke 20:36). They were created to execute His will (Col. 1:16).

> Even after sin entered the world, God's good angels, who did not rebel against Him, are called holy (Mark 8:38). These are the elect angels (1 Tim. 5:21) in contrast to the evil angels who followed Satan in his rebellion against God (Matt. 25:41).
>
> —*Basic Theology*, p. 124

In Revelation 12 we find that one-third of the angels followed Satan. This would mean that two-thirds of the angels remained faithful to their Creator. These are noted as the holy angels, and they remain faithful to the original task for which they were created—attending creation and the throne of God.

If one-third of the angels sinned and followed Satan, then whom do the remaining two-thirds follow? The apocryphal Book of Enoch mentions Michael, Gabriel, Raphael, and Uriel as angel leaders. He adds that there are as many as seven archangels, but only one archangel is mentioned in Scripture: Michael (i.e. Dan. 8:16). If permitted, we might presume that there are three created leaders in the spiritual arena. We have already established that Satan, or Lucifer, is one of these. Who are the other two? It would be unscriptural to state that there is more than one archangel, but there is another prominent angel leader mentioned in Scripture: Gabriel. It would seem feasible that the angels were perhaps divided equally among these three.

The Hebrew meaning of Michael is, "who is like God." Scriptures give us his God-appointed duties, which give an indication of his arena. According to Daniel 10:13, Michael is *one* of the "chief princes." We cannot tell for certain that a chief prince and an archangel are synonymous, but we do read that there is more than one chief prince. "But the prince of the kingdom of Persia withstood me one and twenty days: but, lo, Michael, *one* of the chief princes, came to help me; and I remained there with the kings of Persia." We are given another clue to his sphere of influence in Daniel 12:1: "And at that time shall Michael stand up, the great prince which standeth for the children of thy people." We see that "Daniel distinctly relates Michael to Israel as prince and guardian over the destinies of that nation" (*Pictorial Encyclopedia of the Bible, Vol. 4,* p. 217).

Uriah Smith represents those who believe that the archangel Michael is Christ Himself. Concerning Daniel 10:13, he states:

> Who was Michael, who here came to Gabriel's assistance? The term signifies, "He who is like God," and the Scriptures clearly show that Christ is the one who bears this name. Jude (verse 9) declares that Michael is the Archangel. This word signifies "head, or chief

> angel", and in our text Gabriel calls Him one [or, as the margin reads, *the first*] of the chief princes. There can be but one archangel, and hence it is manifestly improper to use the word in the plural as some do. The Scriptures never so use it. In 1 Thessalonians 4:16, Paul states that when the Lord appears the second time to raise the dead, the voice of the archangel is heard. Whose voice is heard when the dead are raised?—The voice of the Son of God (John 5:28).

Smith is definitely in error when he says that putting these scriptures together (Jude 9; 1 Thess. 4:16; John 5:28), they prove that

> the dead are called from their graves by the voice of the Son of God, that the voice which is then heard is the voice of the Archangel, proving that the Archangel is the Son of God, and that the Archangel is called Michael, from which it follows that Michael is the Son of God.
>
> —*Daniel and the Revelation,* p. 229

The only proof we need to prove that Michael is not the Son of God is in Jude. Michael did not confront the devil over the body of Moses, but rather asked the Lord to intercede. If Michael is God, why did he not command Satan? Also, Michael clearly makes the distinction between himself and the Lord. Smith's view of Michael is certainly in keeping with cult beliefs.

Michael's involvement in the defense of Israel is discussed prophetically in Revelation 12. In verse 7 Michael and his angels—holy angels—are defending Israel from Satan and his angels. "And there was war in heaven: Michael and his angels fought against the dragon; and the dragon fought and his angels." This is a complete turnaround from Jude 9. "Yet Michael the archangel, when contending with the devil he disputed about the body of Moses, durst not bring against him a railing accusation, but said, The Lord rebuke thee." Why did Michael show respect of authority to Satan in Jude 9, and later make war with Satan in Revelation 12? Certainly, on both occasions the welfare of Israel is in view.

Most writers are either silent on this issue or they admit that it is at least a difficult question. We know that Michael was on the offensive and victorious in both instances. In the matter of the body of Moses, it appears to be a one-on-one confrontation. However, Michael could not lower himself to the same level of carnality as Satan, because he was holy—not holy as God is holy, but holy because of his unfallen state. Michael was empowered by the Lord to protect the body of Moses, and that was enough to win the argument. The real question is: Why would the devil want the body of Moses? Although the Bible does not shed any light on this question, there are several possibilities that this writer feels are tenable.

Since the people of Israel had evidently not seen the body of Moses, Satan could have used it to frighten them before they entered into the Promised Land, hoping, I'm sure, to cause them to wander another forty years and perhaps fall once again from the Lord's favor. Satan could have viewed this as a possibility of causing God humiliation. He certainly would have gained satisfaction in abusing the body of the one that defeated him while he remained alive. He might have paraded around toying with the body as a trophy, much as a cat plays with a dead mouse before devouring it. But, the most likely reason is found in Deuteronomy 18:15: "The LORD thy God will raise up unto thee a Prophet from the midst of thee, of thy brethren, like unto me; unto him ye shall hearken." According to Moses himself, he still has a future work, possibly one of the witnesses of Revelation 11.

Michael is also named as a participant in the Rapture of the Church in 1 Thessalonians 4:16: "For the Lord himself shall descend from heaven with a shout, with the voice of the archangel, and with the trump of God: and the dead in Christ shall rise first." Here Michael is seen accompanying the Lord on His return for the Church saints. Evidently, Michael has taken Lucifer's place as the shield and protector of the throne, and accompanies Him wherever He goes. He may be likened to a personal bodyguard who keeps the undesirables from the presence of the king. Satan is not a personal threat to Christ, but his stench is most offensive.

When we see the presence of Michael, we know that the Lord and Satan must be near. In Deuteronomy 34 we read that the Lord took the life of Moses, and in Jude 9 we see that Michael was there contending with Satan. In Daniel 10, as the Lord instructed Daniel, Michael interceded as Satan tried to intervene in the affairs of men. In 1 Thessalonians 4 Michael accompanies Christ at the Rapture, for certainly Satan must be near trying to defeat His plan. In Daniel 12 and Revelation 12 Michael fights as Satan tries to assault the throne of God and His people, Israel. Michael is a holy angel and a powerful soldier of God.

We have already seen that Lucifer was God's most powerful creation. In Isaiah 14:12–20 Satan is called "Lucifer, the son of the morning." Clarence Larkin believes that in Job 38:7 there is a difference between the "morning stars" and the "sons of God." Of Satan, he states:

> This was his glorious title when he was created, and this world of ours was made, at which time—the "Morning Stars" (probably other glorious created ruling beings like himself), sang together, and all the "Sons of God" (angels) shouted for joy.
>
> —*The Book of Revelation*, p. 96

If this is true, and it is quite possible, then there are other creatures like himself, possibly other archangels, with equal or lesser power depending upon the task assigned by the Lord. We know that God enables those whom He creates or calls.

The other likely candidate for being an archangel is Gabriel, the only other good angel mentioned by name in the Bible. His name means "hero of God." His ministry involves giving special messages to men concerning the plans of God. His name appears in only two books of the Bible, Daniel and Luke. Each time he is delivering an important message given to him directly from the mouth of God.

At least one writer thinks that the Gabriel of Daniel 9 is not an angel. He states that

> the narrative of Daniel's vision states clearly that the

> sound heard by Daniel was "voice of a man," so that there is no reason to suppose that this messenger of the Almighty had an appearance of powers apart from man.
>
> —*Pictorial Encyclopedia of the Bible, Vol.* 2, p. 618

This seems unlikely because of the narrative concerning Gabriel in Daniel 9:21: "Yea, whiles I was speaking in prayer, even the man Gabriel, whom I had seen in the vision at the beginning, being caused to fly swiftly, touched me about the time of the evening oblation." This would be the description of an event employing an angel, not a man. Holy angels were often presented in the form of men in the Old Testament and were the messengers used to deliver God's message. They would not be able to be seen in any other form. Added to that, the message and the man appeared in a vision, a common vehicle used by God.

In Luke 1:19 Gabriel once again is the angel to deliver an important message taken directly from the Lord. "And the angel answering said unto him, I am Gabriel, that stand in the presence of God; and am sent to speak unto thee, and to shew thee these glad tidings." Gabriel was the angel that delivered the announcement of the soon coming birth of John the Baptist. The last time we see the name of Gabriel appear in the Bible is in Luke 1:28, with the most important message ever delivered to mankind. This message was delivered to Mary, the soon-to-be mother of our Lord. "And the angel came in unto her, and said, Hail, thou that art highly favoured, the Lord is with thee: blessed art thou among women." With this message came the Hope of mankind, the Savior of the World, Jesus Christ.

In the Old Testament the angels were said to have delivered the law. "For if the word spoken by angels was stedfast, and every transgression and disobedience received a just recompence of reward" (Heb. 2:2). Ryrie says that the phrase "the word spoken by angels," "refers to the Mosaic Law (Ps. 68:17; Acts 7:53). In later Judaism it was held that angels had delivered the law" (*Ryrie Studie Bible,* p. 1853).

The Bible teaches that the holy angels are employed. They are employed in the worship of God, in executing the will of God, and especially in ministering to the heirs of salvation. They are ready to perform any service that will advance the cause of Christ.

> Under the Old Testament they repeatedly appeared to the servants of God to reveal to them his will. They smote the Egyptians; were employed in the giving of the law at Mount Sinai; attended the Israelites during their journey; destroyed their enemies; and encamped around the people of God as a defence in hours of danger. They predicted and celebrated the birth of Christ (Matthew 1:20; Luke 1:11); they ministered to Him in his temptation and sufferings (Matthew 4:11; Luke 22:43); and they announced his resurrection and ascension (Matthew 28:2 John 20:12; Acts 1:10–11). They are still ministering spirits to believers (Hebrews 1:14); they delivered Peter from prison; they watch over children (Matthew 18:10); they bear the souls of the departed to Abraham's bosom (Luke 16:22); they

> are to attend Christ at his second coming, and gather his people into his kingdom (Matthew 13:39; 16:27; 24:31).
>
> —Charles Hodge, *Systematic Theology, Vol. 1,* p. 639

Holy angels have been active in the affairs of God and man since their creation. They live to serve and are spectators observing the events of mankind. They are said to be observing in four instances.

> In Luke 15:10 they are seen beholding the joy of the Lord over one sinner who repents. It is not the joy of the angels, as too often supposed (cf. Jude 1:24). In Luke 12:8–9, the word of Christ is written, "Also I say unto you, Whosoever shall confess me before men, him shall the Son of man also confess before the angels of God: but he that denieth me before men shall be denied before the angels of God." So, also, the whole earth-life of Christ was "seen of angels" (1 Tim. 3:16), and in Revelation 14:10–11, the angels are said to observe the eternal woes of those who "worship the beast and his image." Over against this, the Church, it is predicted, shall judge angels (1 Cor. 6:3), as poorly prepared as they are at present to judge in the least of matters on the earth.
>
> —Lewis Sperry Chafer, *Systematic Theology, Vol. 2,* p. 26

All holy angels worship and serve God. In the spirit world, God has established an order of organization that is strictly observed (Col. 1:16). The holy angels are obedient to those that have been assigned as their leader. The structure of this hierarchy will be addressed later in this endeavor.

The Fallen Angels—Imprisoned

The Fall of Man.

BEELZEBUB'S ADDRESS TO THE FALLEN ANGELS.

"There is a place
(If ancient and prophetic fame in heaven
Err not), another world, the happy seat
Of some new race called Man, about this time
To be created like to us, though less
In power and excellence, but favored more
Of Him who rules above; so was his will
Pronounced among the gods, and by an oath,
That shook heaven's whole circumference, confirmed.
Thither let us bend all our thoughts, to learn
What creatures there inhabit, of what mold
Or substance, how endued, and what their power,
And where their weakness, how attempted best,
By force or subtlety. Though heaven be shut,
And heaven's high Arbitrator sit secure
In his own strength, this place may lie exposed,
The utmost border of his kingdom, left
To their defense who hold it: here, perhaps,
Some advantageous act may be achieved
By sudden onset, either with hell-fire
To waste his whole creation, or possess
All as our own, and drive, as we were driven,
The puny habitants; or, if not drive,

Seduce them to our party, that their God
May prove their foe, and with repenting hand,
Abolish his own works. This would surpass
Common revenge, and interrupt his joy
In our confusion, and our joy upraise
In his disturbance; when his darling sons,
Hurled headlong to partake with us, shall curse
Their frail original and faded bliss,
Faded so soon. Advise, if this be worth
Attempting, or to sit in darkness here
Hatching vain empires." Thus Beelzebub
Pleaded his devilish counsel, first devised
By Satan, and in part proposed; for whence,
But from the author of all ill, could spring
So deep a malice to confound the race
Of mankind in one root, and earth with hell
To mingle and involve, done all to spite
The great Creator? But their spite still serves
His glory to augment. The bold design
Pleased highly those infernal states, and joy
Sparkled in all their eyes with full assent
They vote.

—John Milton, *Paradise Lost*

In the beginning, all angels were created holy. But, at some point in time at least one-third of them fell from their original place, the presence of God. Most certainly the one whom they followed was Lucifer. We do not know when this event happened. We only know that the event took place after the fall of Lucifer. With his fall came the awful disease of sin.

> Sin itself began in heaven with "Lucifer, son of the morning," the highest and most exalted of heaven's created beings, who became Satan when he led a celestial revolt that spread to myriads of the angelic beings (Isa. 14:12–20).
>
> —Merrill E. Unger, *Biblical Demonology,* p. 15

Revelation 12 is a record of the angels that followed Satan. He led one-third of the "stars" (angels) in a revolt against God that caused him to be vanquished from heaven. Some writers believe that at this time God

> "elected" or *permanently confirmed* the holiness of the angels who chose to remain loyal to Him (1 Timothy 5:21). God has apparently given them a special grace of perseverance to enable them to permanently retain their position as holy angels.
>
> —Ron Rhodes, *The Complete Book of Bible Answers,* p. 244

This would seem reasonable because we have no scripture that a subsequent or additional fall occurred. It would also seem logical because the remaining two-thirds had a different leadership that remained loyal to their Creator. The angels ("stars") that followed Lucifer and joined in this revolt are known to Bible students as fallen angels or demons.

In *Systematic Theology, Vol. 2,* Chafer states that "angels were created with the responsibility of self determination." He adds that God was not the instigator of their sin; their fall was anticipated; they were given autonomy to sin or remain sinless; they fell individually; and unlike man whose fall opened the way for redemption, there is no compensating good of any degree in the connection with the fact that the angels sinned.

> These evil spirits are represented as belonging to the same order of beings as the good angels. All the names and titles, expressive of their nature and powers, given to the one are also given to the others. Their original condition was holy. When they fell or what was the nature of their sin is not revealed. The general opinion is that it was pride, founded on 1 Timothy 3:6.
>
> —Charles Hodge, *Systematic Theology, Vol. 1,* p. 643

Some might believe that fallen angels have more or less power than the holy angels.

> The same limitations, of course, belong to their agency as belong to that of the holy angels. (1.) They are dependent on God, and can act only under his control and by his permission. (2.) Their operations must be according to the laws of nature, and, (3.) They cannot interfere with the freedom and responsibility of men.
>
> —Hodge, *Systematic Theology, Vol. 1,* p. 644

Angels are not loose cannons; they are under His control and can only act as He allows.

Some believe that fallen angels and demons are two separate entities. However, Scripture seems to use the terms interchangeably. They are both to be known as evil angels and are normally mentioned in connection with

Satan (Matt. 25:41; Rev. 12:7–9). They are included in the "principality, and power, and might, and dominion" of Ephesians 1:21, and are explicitly mentioned in Ephesians 6:12 and Colossians 2:15. Their chief occupation seems to be that of supporting their leader, Satan, in his warfare against the good angels and God's people and cause. Demons are often mentioned in Scripture, particularly in the Gospels. They are spirit beings (Matt. 8:16), often called "unclean spirits" (Mark 9:25). They serve under the authority of Satan (Luke 11:15–19), though they are ultimately subject to God (Matthew 8:29). Demons are to be equated with fallen angels. They are still free to carry on the work of their leader, Satan.

Unger has this to add about this category:

> Satan holds sway over the fallen spirits, who concurred in his primal rebellion. His authority is without doubt what he has been permitted to retain from his creation. These spirits, having an irrevocable choice to follow Satan, instead of remaining loyal to their Creator, have become irretrievably confirmed in wickedness, and irreparably abandoned to delusion. Hence, they are in full sympathy with their prince, and render him willing service in their varied ranks and positions of service in his highly organized kingdom of evil (Matt. 12:26). Their initial decision has forever wedded them to his deceptive program and also to his inevitable doom.
>
> —*Biblical Demonology,* p. 73

To understand the study of the fallen angels, we must

begin with their leader, Lucifer. In Ezekiel 28:15 we see that he was created perfect. "Thou wast perfect in thy ways from the day that thou wast created, till iniquity was found in thee." We see in this portion of Scripture that Lucifer was created perfect and was the most beautiful creature that God created. He had everything that a creature could possibly have wanted. He had beauty, wisdom, power, and an abode in the very presence of God, with unlimited freedom to all of His creation. Then how and when could this horrible event have taken place?

What was the iniquity or lawlessness found in him? We find the answer to what this sin was in Isaiah 14:11–15:

> Thy pomp is brought down to the grave, and the noise of thy viols: the worm is spread under thee, and the worms cover thee. How art thou fallen from heaven, O Lucifer, son of the morning! how art thou cut down to the ground, which didst weaken the nations! For thou hast said in thine heart, I will ascend into heaven, I will exalt my throne above the stars of God: I will sit also upon the mount of the congregation, in the sides of the north: I will ascend above the heights of the clouds; I will be like the most High. Yet thou shalt be brought down to hell, to the sides of the pit.

The sin that he was guilty of was and is pride. This is the sin that he tempted Adam and Eve with in the garden of Eden. He wanted to be as God, and he instilled this in those in the garden, "and ye shall be as gods" (Gen. 3:5).

His hideous visit to the garden as a fallen creature means that his fall took place sometime between his creation and the fall of man. The fall of the angels also took place somewhere between their creation and the fall of man. This means that the origin of sin originated in the heavens and not on earth. Some place this event between Genesis 1 and 2 and the "darkness" as the result of the chaos of the fall. Many ask the question: Did God create sin?

> Some say that everything that is, is due to God; therefore, he must be the author of sin. To this we reply that if God is the author of evil and condemns the creature for committing sin, we have no moral universe. Others say that evil is due to the nature of the world. The existence of the world is the greatest of all evils and the source of all other evils. Nature itself is evil. But the Scriptures repeatedly declare that all that God made is good and they positively reject the idea that nature is inherently evil (1 Tim. 4:4). And finally, some suggest that evil is due to the nature of the creature. They hold that sin is a necessary stage in the development of the spirit. But the Scriptures speak of no such evolutionary development and look upon the universe and the creatures as originally perfect.
>
> —Henry Theissen, *Lectures in Systematic Theology,* p. 136

God created Lucifer and his angels perfect. Satan and his fallen angels are the product of their own pride and disobedience.

Fallen angels are divided into two separate groups: those that are bound, and those that are free. Those that are bound are imprisoned for some hideous crime that even surpasses the crimes of the other evil angels. Those that are free are called fallen angels or demons. There is no scriptural indication that there is any difference in their calling or activity. Although the Bible does not record the origin of demons, we know through the study of demonology that they exist.

Some believe that demons are the disembodied spirits of a "pre-Adamic race." Scofield is of the opinion that between Genesis 1:1 and 1:2 that some cataclysmic event took place.

> Jer. 4:23–26, Isa. 24:1 and 45:18, clearly indicate that the earth had undergone a cataclysmic change as the result of a divine judgment. The face of the earth bears everywhere the marks of such a catastrophe. There are not wanting intimations which connect it with a previous testing and fall of angels.
>
> —*Scofield Reference Bible,* p. 3

Larkin, a contemporary of Scofield, is in agreement with him. He states that the earth was created in some distant past in a perfect state, and cites Jeremiah 4:23–26 as a proof text. He goes on to say:

> It is clear from the account of the Fall of Adam and Eve that sin existed before man was created. The inference is from Ezek. 28:12–19, Isa. 14:12–14, that when the earth was originally created that Satan was placed

> in charge of it, and that he and his angels rebelled and led astray the inhabitants of the Original Earth, and the Pre-Adamic race are now the demons who as they are permitted liberty seek to re-embody themselves in human beings that they may again dwell on the earth.
>
> —*The Book of Revelation,* p. 195

Although Gaebelein does not hold to the theory of the pre-Adamic race, he does accept the gap theory. He stated that the dwelling place of Lucifer, in his unfallen state, was the earth. He believed that science proved that the earth once existed in a different form than it does now. "There was here a gigantic animal creation and a corresponding gigantic vegetation. Man was not here in that distant past, perhaps millions of years ago." Disputing the scientific claim of the existence of a missing link, he does believe that there was a sudden great judgment of God that wiped out the original creation and plunged it into death, chaos, and darkness. "The condition of the earth as seen in Gen. 1:2 must, therefore, be the result of the fall of Lucifer, when he attempted to have the throne on this globe above the stars" (*The Angels of God,* p. 39).

In *Basic Theology,* Ryrie states that this view understands that Satan originally ruled over a perfect earth and a pre-Adamic race. The sin of Satan somehow involved this race in his rebellion. Upon their death, they lost their bodies and became disembodied spirits or demons. It supports the view that demons are disembodied spirits and seek embodiment. However, he adds that nowhere in the Bible is there even a hint that a pre-

Adamic race ever existed. The inference is that those who hold to the theory of a pre-Adamic race usually teach that demons are "disembodied spirits."

There are, however, many scriptural proofs for the existence of fallen angels or demons as spirit beings, whether imprisoned or free. We should begin with the fallen angels that are imprisoned. The question is: Who are the angels that are imprisoned and why are they imprisoned? The biblical text that demands our attention is 2 Peter 2:4–5:

> For if God spared not the angels that sinned, but cast them down to hell, and delivered them into chains of darkness, to be reserved unto judgment; And spared not the old world, but saved Noah the eighth person, a preacher of righteousness, bringing in the flood upon the world of the ungodly.

The Greek word for hell used here is *Tartarus,* the only time it is found in the New Testament. It is a place of detention until judgment. This text can only describe one event in the Bible, Genesis 6:4.

It would be logical to think that all fallen angels deserve to be imprisoned, but most remain free. For those imprisoned, their sin must be of the most hideous nature. There are three groups that need to be indentified: sons of God, the daughters of men, and giants. Although we cannot be dogmatic in the identity of these groups, we can come to some logical conclusions. The first group to identify is the "sons of God."

Sons of God. The two most recognized identities of

the "sons of God" are the sons of the godly line of Seth and fallen angels. We read in Genesis 6:1–2:

> And it came to pass, when men began to multiply on the face of the earth, and daughters were born unto them, That the sons of God saw the daughters of men that they were fair; and they took them wives of all which they chose.

The subject of this text is the "daughters," not the fathers. The "sons of God" had the power and force to overcome any objection that a father might have. They took what they wanted. We cannot tell by the text if any of these women were already wives, but if so, they too had to accede to whatever the "sons of God" wanted. We have no indication as to exactly when this practice began, except that it happened after the expulsion from the garden and before the flood.

Those that hold to the theory that the "sons of God" were from the godly line of Seth must base their thoughts on the idea that Noah was perfect, and without sin. We know that this cannot be true because of Romans 3:23: "For all have sinned, and come short of the glory of God." Ryrie states: "*all have sinned.* Lit, all sinned, the same verb form as in 5:12, which associates the entire human race with Adam's sin" (*Ryrie Study Bible,* p. 1702). Certainly, this account takes place after the fall was recorded and prior to Genesis 6. At that time, Seth and his descendents had inherited the sin nature.

Alfred Edersheim holds to the Seth theory. He states:

> The corruption of mankind reached its highest point when even the difference between the Sethites and the Cainites became obliterated by intermarriages between the two parties, and that from sensual motives.
> —*Bible History, Old Testament,* p. 27

Robert Jamison also holds to this theory and cites those who hold to the angel theory as those whose "semi-pagan imaginations were dazzled by the rhapsodical legends of the Aprocryphal book of Enoch" (*A Commentary, Vol. 1,* p. 87). He lists Josephus, Justin, Athenagoras, Clemens, Alexandrinus, Tertullian, and Lactantius as early writers with whom he disagreed. These were later opposed by Chrysostom and Augustine. In modern times Rosenmuller, Gesenius, Kurtz, Knobel, Delitzsch, Govett, Maitland, Moore, and Birks espoused the angel theory. Added to the angel theorists were the poets Milton, Byron, and Moore.

One modern writer that has done much in molding opinion is Scofield. Scofield wrote that holding that the "sons of God" were the "angels which kept not their first estate" is a mistake. He maintains that it would be impossible for angels to reproduce based on Matthew 22:30, which says: "For in the resurrection they neither marry, nor are given in marriage, but are as the angels of God in heaven." We would not argue his point that there are no female angels mentioned in Scripture and that angels do not marry. The entire point is irrelevant concerning marriage in heaven. There will be no marriage in heaven because the resurrected saints will not marry. Scofield, as well as the Sadducees, are questioning a condition that could not exist. The Sadducees were beating a dead horse because they did not believe in a resurrection or angels to begin with (Acts 23:8). The sex of the angels is immaterial.

However, his contention that angels are always spoken of in a sexless way is not what we find in Scripture. We find the opposite to be true. Angels are always presented in the masculine gender. Not to belabor the point, we would simply look at one scriptural text to prove the point, Genesis 19. In verse 1, "there came two angels"; he called them "my lords" (masculine) in verse 2; and in verse 5, the men of Sodom called them men. If they were not masculine they fooled even the men in the city that wanted them. The gender of the "sons of God" is found in their name. If the "sons of Gods" in Genesis 6 are angels, they are masculine in gender.

In *Systematic Theology,* Chafer quotes Larkin extensively concerning the "sons of God." Larkin believed that these were angels, but they did not belong to Satan, his reason being that Satan's angels are free and these are bound. He did, however, believe that these angels are bound because of unlawful sexual intercourse committed with human women. This cohabitation with the daughters of Cain produced a godless race.

Finally, the term "sons of God" is used only five times in the Old Testament. It is used twice in Genesis 6:2–4, and three times in Job 1:6, 2:1, and 38:7. In all cases other than Genesis, without exception, it is always accepted as meaning angels. Then why would the meaning of the same word in the Hebrew, *Bne-Ha-Elohim* not be accepted as being the same. If the "sons of God" are men in this passage and we use the law of first mention to guide our interpretation, we are bound to use Genesis 6 to interpret the other three places as being men and not angels.

It is therefore my conclusion that the "sons of God" are fallen angels and are synonymous with the "angels that sinned" in 2 Peter 2:4. This, I believe, is the best and only interpretation of the text in Genesis 6:4 and 2 Peter 2:4 that is in harmony with all other scripture and violates no rule of interpretation.

Daughters of Men. There is little contention over the identity of the "daughters of men," *Bnoth-Ha-Adam.* In fact, most writers fail to hardly mention them at all. They are, however, very important in the formula producing "giants." As far as Scripture is concerned, angels are never presented in any way but male; therefore the "daughters of men" are not seriously thought of as angels.

Some believe that Zechariah 5 is speaking of female angels. However, the text seems to eliminate that possibility. In verse 9:

> Then lifted I up mine eyes, and looked, and, behold, there came out two women, and the wind was in their wings; for they had wings like the wings of a stork: and they lifted up the ephah between the earth and the heaven.

They are called women with wings, not angels with wings. I'm sure the writer was adept enough in Hebrew to say what he meant, because he spoke to an angel in verse 10. They were probably agents of evil because they represented one of the unclean birds of Leviticus 11:19.

It is interesting to note in our text that nothing is said

of giant women, which would have been the case if the sons of Seth married the daughters of Cain. Adam was created in the likeness of God and his descendents were born in his likeness. However, if the "sons of God" were the godly line of Seth, then why were the offspring called "giants"? There was something different about their children; they did not even appear as normal men. There is little to be said about the "daughters of men," except that they were indeed daughters.

Nothing is said of any resistance on the part of the parents or the daughters. Were these women seduced by these fallen angels or were they possessed, which rendered any resistance moot? Were the parents afraid, or had they lowered themselves to the level of the beast and simply allowed them to have their way? Perhaps their wickedness had brought them to a place of worshipping these demons. How many women were involved and the number of offsprings they produced are questions not answered in Scripture.

We must conclude that the "daughters of men" were human women and in no way can they be construed as angels. They could be Cainite daughters, but it still would not affect the identity of the "sons of God."

Giants. The last group to be discussed is the giants, *Hans-Nephilim.* We read in Genesis 6:4:

> There were giants in the earth in those days; and also after that, when the sons of God came in unto the daughters of men, and they bare children to them, the same became mighty men which were of old, men of renown.

Coupled with 2 Peter 2:4, it is certain that the main contributing factor for the wickedness of man and the ultimate destruction by the flood was the cohabiting of angels with human women. This cohabitation produced an offspring that the King James Version denotes as "giants" (Hebrew, *nephilim*). We see that their appearance takes place in two different time periods, a time before the flood and a time after the flood (Num. 13:33). If these giants died during the flood, and the angels that produced them were imprisoned at the flood, how could they reappear? Did this event happen again after the flood, or is there another possible explanation?

Unger states:

> The Septuagint translators' rendering of the expression by "giants" (*gigantes*) seems clearly an indication that they thought of the *nephilim* in this passage and its only other occurrence in Numbers 13:33 as the offspring of the sons of God (angels) and the daughters of men (mortal women); for the basic idea of the Greek term is not monstrous size, which is a secondary and developed meaning, but *gegenes*, "earth-born," and employed of the Titans who were partly of celestial and partly of terrestrial origin.
>
> —*Biblical Demonology,* p. 48

So the translators of the Septuagint reject the idea that these offspring were giant in stature, but hold to the angel theory. They instead hold more to the mythological ideas. According to Unger, they held to the idea that the "fallen ones" were a mixture of human and angel, much as the rebellious Titans.

C. F. Keil does not accept the angel theory or the fact that the "giants" were their offspring, but refuses to be dogmatic in his assessment.

> *"The same were mighty men"*: this might point back to the *Nephilim,* but it is a more natural supposition, that it refers to the children born to the sons of God. *"These," i.e.* the sons sprung from those marriages, *"are the heroes, those renowned heroes of old."* Now if, according to the simple meaning of the passage, the *Nephilim* were in existence at the very time when the sons of God came in to the daughters of men, the appearance of the *Nephilim* cannot afford the slightest evidence that the "sons of God" were angels, by whom a family of monsters were begotten, whether demigods, demons, or angel-men.
>
> —*Commentary on the Old Testament, Vol. 1,* p. 138

Robert Jamison also believes that the giants, or nephilim, were already in existence prior to the offspring of the "sons of God" and the "daughters of men." He adds that the only other scripture that mentions giants is Numbers 13:32–33. Here the root meaning of the words suggest the idea of extraordinary size. He added that in keeping with the antediluvian size of other animals such as quadrupeds and other inferior animals, it would be quite normal for man to be equally large in size. In fact, he states that they would be immensely larger than today's counterpart. "The analogy of nature would require that 'man amongst the mammoths' should, in physique, have borne some proportion to the magnitude of his bestial contemporaries" (*A Commentary, Vol. 1,* p. 89).

In other words, they were physical "giants." They were physically larger, but it was a natural phenomenon dictated by the era in which they lived. However, the same reasoning would not explain the size difference demonstrated in the report of spies that Moses sent into the Promised Land. There were definitely people that were much larger than the spies, and which had made them afraid. If this line of reasoning were to prevail, there should be evidence of their existence alongside the remains of the giant animals. Whatever the meaning of "giants," something made them stand out from the rest of the inhabitants. There was something different about them. The best option is that there were those that were physical giants.

Josephus, the Jewish historian, followed the constant opinion of antiquity that the fallen angels were the fathers of old giants. He states:

> Whereby they made God to be their enemy, for many angels of God accompanied with women, and begat sons that proved unjust, and despisers of all that was good, on account of the confidence they had in their own strength; for the tradition is, That these men did what resembled the acts of those whom the Grecians call giants.
>
> —*Antiquities of the Jews,* p. 73

Philo also follows the same constant opinion of antiquity.

> On what principle it was that giants were born of angels and women (Genesis 6:4)? The poets call those

> men who were born out of the earth giants, that is to say, sons of the earth. But Moses here uses this appellation improperly, and he uses it too very often merely to denote the vast personal size of the principal men, equal to that of Hajk or Hercules. But he relates that these giants were sprung from a combined procreation of two natures, namely, from angels and mortal women.
>
> —*The Works of Philo,* p. 811

Philo questions Moses' use of the word giant, but not the fact that he used giant to denote physical size. He, as well as the other ancients, favor the idea that the product of the angels and women were in fact physical giants.

The last of the ancients that we will note is "The Book of Enoch."

> **Chapter 15**
>
> 1. Then addressing me, He spoke and said: Hear, neither be afraid, O Enoch, O righteous man, and scribe of righteousness: approach hither, and hear my voice. Go, say to the Watchers of heaven, who have sent thee to pray for them, You ought to pray for men, and not men for you.
>
> 2. Wherefore have you forsaken the lofty and holy heaven, which endures for ever, and have lain with women; have defiled yourselves with the daughters of men; have taken to yourselves wives; have acted like the sons of the earth, and have begotten giants? [see Gen. 6:2,4]

3. You being spiritual, holy, and living a life which is eternal, have polluted yourselves with women; have begotten in carnal blood; have lusted in the blood of men; and have done as those who are flesh and blood do.

4. These however die and perish.

5. Therefore have I given to them wives, that they might cohabit with them; that sons might be born of them; and that this might be transacted upon earth.

6. But you from the beginning were made spiritual, possessing a life which is eternal, and not subject to death in all the generations of the world.

7. Therefore I made not wives for you, because, being spiritual, your dwelling is in heaven [Matt. 22].

8. Now the giants, who have been born of spirit and of flesh, shall be called upon earth evil spirits, and on earth shall be their habitation. Evil spirits shall proceed from their flesh, because they were created from above; from the holy Watchers was their beginning and primary foundation. Evil spirits shall they be upon earth, and the spirits of the wicked shall they be called. The habitation of the spirits of heaven shall be in heaven; but upon earth shall be the habitation of terrestrial spirits, who are born on earth [1 Cor. 15:40].

9. The spirits of the giants shall be like clouds, which shall oppress, corrupt, fall, contend, and bruise upon earth.

10. They shall cause lamentation. No food shall they eat; and they shall be thirsty; they shall be concealed, and those spirits shall not rise up against the sons of men, and against women; for they come forth

[from them] during the days of slaughter and destruction [Lk. 4:33, 36; Matt. 8:28-34].

Chapter 16

1. And as to the death of the giants, wheresoever their spirits depart from their bodies, let their flesh, that which is perishable, be without judgment. Thus shall they perish, until the day of the great consummation of the great world. It shall be consummated respecting the Watchers and the impious.

2. And now to the Watchers, who have sent thee to pray for them, who in the beginning were in heaven,

3. Say, In heaven have you been; secret things however, have not been manifested to you; yet have you known a reprobated mystery.

4. And this you have related to women in the hardness of your heart, and by that mystery have women and mankind multiplied evils upon the earth [Jude 4, 6, 13].

5. Say to them, Never therefore shall you obtain peace.

—*Book of Enoch,* chapters 15 and 16 [54]

The decision as to whether the "sons of God" were fallen angels or the sons of the ungodly line of Cain is a decision of conviction. All are guilty of basing some interpretation on preconceived ideas and sometimes mistaken conclusions. We are sometimes forced to render a verdict in such a way as not to violate another personal doctrine or belief. This is not one of the dogmatics and therefore should not be a point of contention among the students of the Bible. It is, however, a challenge that demands a logical line of thinking which is constant throughout our basic statement of faith.

It is also my conclusion that the "giants" were offspring produced by the cohabitation of fallen angels and earthly women. This cohabitation is the only known instance of its kind in Scripture. Genesis 6:4 does state that "there were giants in the earth in those days; and also after that, when the sons of God came in unto the daughters of men, and they bare children to them." Can "after that" refer to the account of giants such as Goliath in 1 Samuel 17:4 or in Numbers 13, when the spies told of men of great stature, which were giants, the sons of Anak? It is curious as to how this happened.

When the Hebrew children, under the leadership of Moses, arrived at the Jordan River, they were instructed to spy out the land. Upon returning from the reconnaissance, they had good news and bad news. The good news was the report of the size of the fruit and the goodness of the land. The bad news was that the good news paled in comparison to the size of the inhabitants. Was this by Satan's design or was it just their misfortune? Where did these giants come from and what were they doing in Israel's path?

Moses wrote both reports on giants, both before and after the flood. I'm sure that when he was writing the report in Genesis he was thinking about his experience at the Jordan River: "There were giants in the earth in those days; and also after that." The possible implication in Genesis 6 is that the giants before the flood were somehow connected with these giants in the land. Was there another event of cohabitation between angels and women? If this is the case, then perhaps it can happen again during the Tribulation. It is also possible that these giants were a product of the genes carried beyond the flood by Noah's wife or daughters-in-law.

We read in Genesis 6:8–9: "But Noah found grace in the eyes of the Lord. These are the generations of Noah: Noah was a just man and perfect in his generations, and Noah walked with God." A note in the *Ryrie Study Bible* says that this means "mature or well–rounded, though not sinless." While we agree that Noah was a mature and reasonable man, the term "generations" adds another dimension to the equation. Generation has to do with his genealogy, not perfection. His genealogy was not mingled with the cohabitation of angels and women. His bloodline was pure and free from the mixture. In verse 10 it is added: "And Noah begat three sons, Shem, Ham, and Japheth." We conclude that his three sons carried the same pure genes that their father carried. We would also conclude that if his three sons were of pure blood, then Noah's wife would also be purebred.

However, Scripture says nothing about the generations of the wives of Noah's three sons. If the giants in the Promised Land and the sons of Anak were the product of natural genes, then they received them through one of the children of Shem, Ham, or Japheth. We would conclude from Genesis 10:6 that the son most likely would be Ham. Ham's son Canaan settled the area known as the Promised Land. The opponents of the angel theory could well use the same approach to prove their theory. If the wives of Noah's three sons were from the lineage of Cain, their genes could have been carried beyond the flood to produce giants. However, based on the evidence and presentation of Scripture this is less likely. We should now take a brief look at the fallen angels that are free.

Fallen Angels That Remain Free

Those angels that followed Lucifer and are free today serve their master, Satan. They have been, and continue to be, active in the lives of men under the direction of Satan. Satan is an angel and described as the prince of demons in Matthew 12:24: "But when the Pharisees heard it, they said, This fellow doth not cast out devils, but by Beelzebub the prince of the devils." The term used here is "devils." However, the word that appears in the original Greek is *daimonia,* demons. The original Greek word for devil is *diabolos.* In verse 26, Jesus does not dispute that Beelzebub was the prince of demons, but actually validifies it with His comparison of Satan with Satan's kingdom. This gives us proof that the devil is in charge of the "demons" that remained free and are still active after the incarceration in Genesis 6.

While the activity of "demons" or "fallen angels" are active in the Old Testament, there are only a few narratives concerning their activity. One notable instance is in Daniel 10:13: "But the prince of the kingdom of Persia withstood me one and twenty days: but, lo, Michael, one of the chief princes, came to help me; and I remained there with the kings of Persia." This Divine messenger had been detained by a more powerful fallen angel.

Clearly, this narrative shows that fallen angels were active at that time.

Other Old Testament passages that prove the activity of fallen angels or demons include Leviticus 17: 7 and Deuteronomy 32:17, where Israel was forbidden to sacrifice to devils; 2 Chronicles 11:15, where Jeroboam had ordained priests for the devils; Psalm 106:36–37, where they were sacrificing their sons and daughters to devils; and Isaiah 13:21 and 34:14, which speaks of satyrs or possible demons.

The activity of fallen angels is always present where God's people are involved. Where God is advancing, Satan and his angels are on the defensive. They are always there trying to thwart the work of the Almighty. Satan, with the aid of his angels, is always on the lookout for those who can be enlisted into his cause. Although there are many other instances of fallen angelic activity in the Old Testament, most of the cases are noted in the New Testament. We will mention the New Testament activity in a later chapter.

Chapter Four

The Organization and Personalities of Angels

The very word for world is *kosmos* and means orderly arrangement. Every part of God's creation was created in an orderly arrangement, including the spirit world of angels. There are many different orders of ranking in the spirit world, and each were apparently assigned a task. It is evident that God originally organized all the angels. However, since Lucifer's fall, the fallen angels have been reassigned by Lucifer himself. They have turned order into chaos in both creation and in the creature, and are determined to interrupt every corner of God's universe. The angels' rule of power and authority are arranged into a pyramid of sorts, with the most powerful at the top and the least powerful at the bottom. It seems that the more the power, the less in number. The rankings of the angels are the same whether they or holy or fallen.

The highest ranking angel in creation is Lucifer (or Satan) as seen in Ezekiel 28:12: "Thou sealest up the sum, full of wisdom, and perfect in beauty." He is at the top of the pyramid. He is followed by the archangel Michael, and another powerful angel, Gabriel. Since we have already discussed them previously, we will forego any discussion concerning them at this time. We will then discuss the other types of angels in the pyramid.

Seraphim

The first order is the "seraphim." The word *seraphim* means "burning ones." Isaiah 6:2, 6 describes the seraphim as they stood above the throne of God.

> Above it stood the seraphims: each one had six wings; with twain he covered his face, and with twain he covered his feet, and with twain he did fly. . . . Then flew one of the seraphims unto me, having a live coal in his hand, which he had taken with the tongs from off the altar.

Their duty was to attend the throne of God and were agents of cleansing. *Strong's Exhaustive Concordance* says that the word comes from the Hebrew *saraph,* meaning "burning," figuratively a fiery (serpent). In the *Pictorial Dictionary of the Bible,* seraphim has the meaning of "princes" or "nobles." In *Commentary on the Old Testament, Vol. 1,* Delitzsch says that the name cannot possibly be connected with the word snake. He adds that the true meaning is "to set on fire" or "to burn up."

The same word for "fiery serpents" in Isaiah 6:2 is used of the creatures in Numbers 21:6. "And the LORD sent fiery serpents among the people, and they bit the people; and much people of Israel died." However, most writers agree that this is a poisonous snake with a burning lethal bite and is not the same thing we see in Isaiah.

It is likely that Lucifer is also a seraphim. We first read of the "serpent" in Genesis 3:1: "Now the serpent was more subtil than any beast of the field which the LORD God had made. And he said unto the woman, Yea, hath God said, Ye shall not eat of every tree in the garden?" Satan was working from experience. He himself had already experienced rejection by God for trying to become "as God." He knew what the outcome would be: expulsion from the garden and the presence of God, as he was expelled from heaven and the presence of God.

Why did Satan work through the serpent?

> Apparently a beautiful creature, in its uncursed state, that Satan used in the temptation. *more subtil.* i.e., clever, not in a degrading sense at this point. *he said.* Satan spoke through the serpent. Perhaps Eve did not realize that animals could not speak; at any rate, she was not alarmed.
>
> —*Ryrie Study Bible,* p. 8

The curse that followed signifies that this was not a common serpent as seen today.

Hodge states that the serpent was neither a figurative designation nor a form of Satan. He writes:

> A real serpent was the agent of the temptation, as it is plain from what is said of the natural characteristics of the serpent in the first verse of the chapter, and from the curse pronounced upon the animal itself, and the

> enmity which was declared should subsist between it and man through all time.
>
> —*Systematic Theology,* p. 127

He adds that Satan was the real tempter, and the serpent was merely an instrument to be used that did not contain the high intellectual faculties that the tempter displayed. Also:

> As to the serpent's speaking there is no more difficulty than in the utterance of articulate words from Sinai, or the sounding of a voice from heaven at the baptism of our Lord, or in the speaking of Balaam's ass. The words uttered were produced by the power of Satan, and of such effects produced by angelic beings good and evil there are numerous instances in the Bible.

The entire form of the serpent was obviously changed. It was reduced to crawl on its belly and to eat dust all the days of its life. We then see something very curious take place. God cursed the serpent and lowered its position to below that of cattle. This leads us to think that the serpent was a willing subject, or that the serpent was Satan himself, not a serpent possessed by Satan. However, it was no mere serpent as we know them today, because the curse and prophecy was placed on an intelligent creature in verse 15. "And I will put enmity between thee and the woman, and between thy seed and her seed; it shall bruise thy head, and thou shalt bruise his heel."

In Revelation 12:9, we again see Satan called a serpent. "And the great dragon was cast out, that old serpent, called the Devil, and Satan." Again in 20:2: "And he laid hold on the dragon, that old serpent, which is the Devil, and Satan, and bound him a thousand years." Although he is never actually called a seraphim, his responsibility of attending the throne of God mentioned in Ezekiel 28:14 in context with his being a cherub seems to indicate that possibility. Some believe that Habbakuk 1:14 is speaking of Satan, the serpent. "And makest men as the fishes of the sea, as the *creeping things,* that have no ruler over them?" According to *Strong's Exhaustive Concordance,* the Hebrew term for "creeping things" is *remes,* meaning "a reptile or any other rapidly moving animal." This must mean the serpent and reptile kingdom. We know that Satan is a serpent, and at the fall possibly lost his position as leader of this kingdom.

The seraphim are exclusive humanlike creatures and are not mentioned apart from Isaiah 6. They are spirit beings and messengers, therefore they qualify as angels. They apparently have an enormous amount of power, and their responsibility seems only to involve proximity to the throne of God. Unlike the cherubim they are said to have only one face, but like the cherubim they are said to have six wings. The number of seraphim is unknown. We know that there are more than one because of verses 2, 3, and 6 indicating plurality, i.e., "Then flew one of the seraphims [plural] unto me."

Cherubim

Like the seraphim, the "cherubim" are also strange creatures. They too are spirit beings and messengers and qualify as angels. However, they seem to be more prolific in scope than the seraphim. They are mentioned some ninety-four times in Scripture as opposed to the single text of seraphim.

We know that the cherubim are high ranking angels because Satan is described as one in Ezekiel 28:14–16:

> Thou art the anointed cherub that covereth; and I have set thee so: thou wast upon the holy mountain of God; thou hast walked up and down in the midst of the stones of fire. Thou wast perfect in thy ways from the day that thou wast created, till iniquity was found in thee. By the multitude of thy merchandise they have filled the midst of thee with violence, and thou has sinned: therefore I will cast thee as profane out of the mountain of God: and I will destroy thee, O covering cherub, from the midst of the stones of fire.

Apparently, his consecration placed him as the leader of the cherubs, the guardians of the throne. His lofty position caused his heart to fill with pride and he fell. It is not known if any other cherubim followed him in his insurrection.

Cherubs were placed at the entrance to the garden of Eden: "So he drove out the man; and he placed at the east of the garden of Eden Cherubims, and a flaming sword which turned every way, to keep the way of the tree of life" (Gen. 3:24). Under God's orders, these powerful spirit beings kept Adam and Eve, as well as all those who followed, from access to the "tree of life." In Revelation 22:2, we read of the reappearance of the "tree of life."

There is no need for cherubs as guardians in the New Jerusalem because sin will have been eradicated and eternity established. The tree of life will then be made accessible to its inhabitants.

The cherubim were also used as decorations in the Tabernacle and Temple. In describing the mercy seat W. G. Moorehead states:

> Its lid, or covering, was a slab of pure gold, held firmly in its place by the crown of gold (elevated edges of the ark) into which it was closely fitted. This covering was the Mercy-seat. From its ends rose the Cherubim, which were formed out of the gold of the mercy-seat itself, not separate attachments. Their wings were projected over their heads and forward, thus forming a sort of canopy for the ark. Their faces were turned toward each other, their eyes bent downward toward the mercy-seat. Two things are very manifest with respect to them: First, they are intimately associated with the throne of God. Both Ezekiel and John in the Apocalypse make this clear. Even in the ark they are connected with the throne, for such the ark was. Second, they are closely connected with the judicial government of the Most High, and appear to be executors of the divine will.
>
> —*The Tabernacle,* p. 283

Ridout, in viewing the Ark of the Covenant, says:

> Their employment is worship rather than judgment. They were the symbols of the host of heaven, the an-

> gels, ministers of divine judgment and justice, associated with God as His servants in His government of the world. As such, they are His representatives, vested with His authority and, so far as needed, with His power. These figures would suggest competent witness to God's holiness, righteousness and goodness.
>
> —*Lectures on the Tabernacle,* p. 77

I. M. Haldeman states that the "shekinah light" shined forth between the figures of the cherubim:

> The Cherubim were on the Mercy Seat and formed an essential part of it. You could not separate the cherubim from the Mercy Seat. The Cherubim represent supremacy over the natural powers. They symbolize all power.
>
> —*The Tabernacle Priesthood and Offerings,* p. 176

In the Tabernacle, cherubim were embroidered on ten curtains of fine white twisted linen and other materials of blue, purple, and scarlet. These curtains were twenty-eight cubits by four cubits each. When joined together they covered the entire outside wall of the Tabernacle (Exod. 26:1; 38:8). The veil separating the holy place and the most holy place was made of the same material and also contained embroidered cherubim (Exod. 26:31; 36:35).

In Solomon's Temple, in the inner sanctuary, there were two olive-wood cherubim overlaid with gold (1 Kings 6:23–28; 2 Chron. 3:10–14; 5:7–9). They were ten cubits high and each had two wings five cubits long with a wingspread of ten cubits each. They were facing the entrance of the Temple so that the outside tips of their wings touched the outside walls, and the inside tips touched each other's wingtip. On the wood paneled walls were carved figures of cherubim, palm trees, and open flowers in both the inner and outer rooms (1 Kings 6:29; 2 Chron. 3:7). These figures were also carved into the olive-wood doors of the sanctuary, and the cypress doors of the nave. These figures were overlaid with gold. Solomon made bronze laver stands patterned after a chariot (1 Kings 7:27–39). Each had four wheels with attached panels and decorations of lions, oxen, cherubim, and wreaths. These same decorations were carved into the round band at the top of the base.

In Ezekiel's Temple (Ezek. 41:17–20), cherubim were an important part of the decoration theme. Cherubim and palms trees were carved all around the inner wall, the nave, and from the floor to above the top of the door. The cherubim had two faces that were turned to opposite directions. The cherubim and the palm trees were alternated.

The description and activity of the cherubim in Ezekiel 10 is one of the strangest in the entire Bible. This narrative is very difficult to comprehend and therefore has been the subject of everything from songs to scriptural proof of extraterrestrial space vehicles. They are called "living creatures" by Ezekiel and seem to closely match the description given by John in Revelation 4, which he also calls "living creatures." Although they are not called cherubim in Revelation, we would assume them to at least be like those in Ezekiel, although not exactly the same creatures. Both occurrences find the "living creatures serving around and in the midst of the throne of God."

There are some differences in the description of the creatures in the two narratives. In Ezekiel 10 the cherubim are described as having the likeness of a man, with each having four faces, four wings, feet like calve's feet, and hands like a man's hands under their wings on all four sides. Their four faces were all different. The first face was that of a cherub; the second, that of a man; the third, that of a lion; and the fourth, that of an eagle. In addition they were escorted by wheels wherever they went. In verse 20 Ezekiel states that he knows that these are cherubim. Also, in Ezekiel's vision, the cherubims traveled on wheels.

In John's vision the faces were similar. They had six wings instead of four, and they had no wheels. In *The Book of Revelation* Larkin explains this is the permanent home of the cherubim, therefore they no longer need wheels. However, because these are spirit beings and are not limited by physical dimensions, we must assume that these wheels are not for mobility.

Larkin relates these creatures to the standards of Israel as to their position as they were stationed in the wilderness. The camp of Judah, representing three tribes that rested on the east, was represented by the likeness of a lion. The camp of Ephraim, representing three tribes that rested on the west, was represented by the likeness of an ox. The camp of Reuben, representing three tribes that rested on the south, was represented by the likeness of a man. Finally, the camp of Dan, representing three tribes that rested on the north, was represented by the likeness of an eagle. He concludes that the Tabernacle is in the center of the camp surrounded and protected by the standards that bore the figures of Ezekiel's and John's vision.

Larkin agrees with Joseph Seiss in his assessment of the different faces of the cherubim representing the four camps of Israel. Each face looked to a different direction and did not turn regardless of what direction they were moving. Seiss states that this is the exact way that the camp of Israel moved. They were formed with four sides like unto a square. When they moved, they moved as a square without turning. This would mean that at times different sides would be the leader depending on the direction they were moving.

Seiss also mentions explanations offered by others that cannot fulfill the real meaning of the verses. One states that some took these to be the four evangelists. However, Seiss says that the four evangelists were Jews and the living creatures are from all tribes, tongues, peoples, and nations. Some interpret this to be the redeemed in general, but it is too indefinite to fill the requirements of the vision. Others view this as representing different dispensations: the lion, the patriarchal; the ox, the Mosaic; the man, the Christian; and the eagle, the millennial. But Seiss points out that these are living beings and that they existed before the dispensations and were actually participating in their introduction.

Seiss concludes that the "living creatures" or "cherubim" of Ezekiel 10 and the "living creatures" of Revelation 4 are not the same creatures.

> They sing precisely the same song (chap. 5:9–10) which the Elders sing. They give praise to the Lamb for having died for them, and for redeeming them by His blood "out of every tribe, and tongue, and people, and nation." They say to the Lamb, "Thou *redeemest* us to God by Thy blood." This settles the point that they are also glorified men, not "beasts" at all, nor mere personifications of mute creation or nature's forces.
>
> —*The Apocalypse,* p. 106

Seiss then presents additional proof that the "living creatures" are not the same in both texts. He mentions that the cherubim of Genesis 3:24 were not men because no other men existed; there was only Adam and Eve. Ezekiel's cherubim could not have been men because there were not men glorified at this time. However, the "living creatures" at the time of John were men.

> They are redeemed men, glorified, and related to the judgment-throne in heaven, and to the interests and affairs of the future kingdom on earth, as the cherubim are related to the throne and kingdom now, and in the former dispensations.

He goes on to state these are the cherubim of the new order. "They have wings, for they are angelic now; and more wings than their angelic predecessors, showing how fully they are capacitated for motion, and how much wider is the sphere of their movements."

John Walvoord states that the four beasts of Revelation 4 can be considered as different aspects of Divine majesty. They are all supreme in their respective categories.

> The lion is king of beasts and represents majesty and omnipotence. The calf or ox, representing the most important of domestic animals, signifies patience and continuous labor. Man is the greatest of all God's creatures, especially in intelligence and rational power; whereas the eagle is greatest among birds and is symbolic of sovereignty and supremacy.
>
> —*The Revelation of Jesus Christ,* p. 109

Although we may agree that the cherubim or living creatures of Ezekiel 10 and Revelation 4 may differ in description and ministry, the best conclusion as to their identity is that of angels. The description of the living creatures may or may not be cherubim in both cases, but they are similar and both attend the throne of God. The fact that these creatures have six wings, as do the seraphim of Isaiah 6, adds to the conclusion that they are angels. Angels are mentioned more often in prophetic passages such as Isaiah, Ezekiel, and Revelation. There may be many different kinds of this type of angel that are not discussed in the Bible. We have yet to see and hear all the wonderful things that God has prepared for us in heaven. E. W. Bullinger reaches no conclusion. He simply states: "In brief, then, we may say that the cherubim are heavenly realities; living ones of whom we know nothing by experience" (*Commentary on Revelation,* p. 226).

These are, however, one of the two types described in Scripture that actually have wings. We therefore reach the same conclusion as Walvoord that the best explanation is that these creatures are angels.

Chief Princes

The "chief princes" are the next group of angels according to the power and authority structure. The only scripture we find this designation is in Daniel 10:13: "But the prince of the kingdom of Persia withstood me one and twenty days: but, lo, Michael, one of the *chief princes,* came to help me; and I remained there with the kings of Persia." Michael is elsewhere listed as an archangel in Jude 9. He is the only archangel mentioned in Scripture. Therefore, we can rightfully conclude that there is more than one archangel, because there is more than one chief prince. This would give credence to the earlier conclusion that Lucifer and Gabriel may also be archangels as well as chief princes.

Here we see angels involved in the control of nations. The "prince of the kingdom of Persia" is also an angel, but apparently not as powerful, and not a chief prince. This shows the hierarchy of angels. With the chief prince's help, the angel was then able to remain with the evil angels and hold his own. The work of this archangel is to be involved in the affairs of Israel and aid those assigned to assist in the affairs of Israel.

In *A Commentary on the Old Testament, Vol. 2,* A. R. Fausset makes a good point in his observation concerning the phrase, "and I remained there with the kings of Persia." These evil angels were trying to prevent the Jews returning to Jerusalem. The holy angel was there pleading on Israel's behalf and losing the argument. Michael came and persuaded the evil angels to favor Israel. The angel was then capable of staying behind and defending the Jews because of the intervention of the chief prince. As Lehman Strauss points out in *The Prophecies of Daniel* concerning Daniel 10, Jude 9, and Revelation 12, the chief prince and archangel Michael is always involved in warfare between good and evil angels.

Princes

In Daniel 10 we read a narrative that tells a great deal about how the matter of prayer involves angels. Daniel had received a vision that disturbed him very much. He began to pray and fast for an answer to his vision. He prayed and fasted for twenty-one days before he received an answer. We notice several things that help us understand the relationship between the one praying and the angel that was sent to deliver God's message.

Daniel went three weeks without a decent meal or even a bath. He was serious. Finally, the answer came in the form of an angel. The angel had a formidable appearance. He begins his description in verse 5. He was clothed in fine linen and a golden girdle; his body appeared as the color of beryl, and his face as lightning; his eyes as lamps of fire; his arms and feet were the color of polished brass; and, his voice had the volume of a multitude. His appearance was frightening and Daniel acted accordingly; he was terrified. This is the normal biblical reaction to an angel, not the casual beginning of a conversation, as told by those today who claim to have experienced an angel's visit.

The angel's appearance was selective; only Daniel saw him (vs. 7). "And I Daniel alone saw the vision: for the men that were with me saw not the vision; but a great quaking fell upon them, so that they fled to hide themselves." Daniel's companions were frightened by the very presence of the angel. Did these men feel the very presence of an angel or could they hear his words? This very thing happened to Saul on the road to Damascus. He was frightened by what he saw, and the men with him were frightened by the words that came from above. They too never saw what Saul was experiencing.

In verse 10 we see that the angel made physical contact with Daniel: "And, behold, an hand touched me, which set me upon my knees and upon the palms of my hands." In the New Testament we see something similar. In Acts 12 Peter was arrested by Herod and cast into prison. An angel from the Lord came to Peter in prison and "smote him on the side" (vs. 7). In both instances an angel was sent to one of God's faithful as an answer to prayer, and in both cases the angels touched them to get their attention. We see here that angels have worked the same in both testaments, under Law and under grace. Today Christians call this a visit by a guardian angel.

In Daniel 10:12 we see that our prayers are heard immediately: "Fear not, Daniel: for from the first day that thou didst set thine heart to understand, and to chasten thyself before thy God, thy words were heard, and I am come for thy words." Not only were his prayers heard, but an angel was sent to Daniel in answer to his prayer.

However, as the angel was on his way to Daniel's

aid, "the prince of the kingdom of Persia" detained him. The "prince of the kingdom of Persia" could only be an angel and not mere man. Why? Because only an angel could interfere with another angel. The "prince" would have to be of a higher rank in order to detain Daniel's angel. He would also be an evil angel, because a holy angel would not interfere in the mission of an angel sent by God. Here we also see that the rank of angels is still in place—both holy and evil. An evil angel of higher rank detained a holy angel of lesser rank. We also see this in the argument between Satan and Michael over the body of Moses in Jude 9.

Daniel's angel, being detained by a stronger angel, needed the help of an angel stronger than a prince. It took Michael, a chief prince and archangel, to break the deadlock. Why Satan did not come to the aid of his prince is not known. Perhaps he was detained elsewhere and could not attend, not being omniscient. Or perhaps God disallowed his interference. After Michael interceded, Daniel's angel was left in charge of the situation, given the authority by Michael. Although the Bible does not say, it does strongly imply that there is honor among the angels for even their enemies. It would be like unto the officers in opposing armies. Even though they are enemies, they have a respect for those of equal or higher rank. The prince of Persia respected the rank of Michael, even though he represented an opposing army, and respected his decision which allowed an angel of lesser rank to stand in for him.

In Jude 9 Michael the archangel did not disrespect an angel of higher rank, Satan. However, when the Lord interceded he gained the advantage and won the argument. In Revelation 12 Michael is ordered into battle because of Satan's assault against Israel. Satan has entered Michael's arena, and he is defending his home ground. Satan and his forces were repelled and could not return to the presence of God in heaven. Michael honored the orders and responsibilities of the Lord, his superior, which has nothing to do with respect of the enemy.

It is not divulged in the text why it took Michael twenty-one days to come to the angel's aid. Perhaps it was to test Daniel's resolve and strengthen him for future battles. After the angel encouraged and strengthened Daniel, he told him that he must return to do battle again with the "prince of Persia." He adds that after he again joins in the fight with this prince, he would then be assaulted by another angel, the "prince of Grecia." These princes are nothing more than demons that are assigned by Satan to interfere in the affairs of governments. The text seems to bear out that there are demons assigned to every government. Strauss asks:

> Was the angel telling Daniel that after the conflict with the prince of Persia he was going to engage in combat with another demon, namely "the prince of Grecia"? That is exactly right! At the time the angel spoke this word to Daniel, the Medo-Persian Empire had about two hundred years yet to run before the rise of Greece. Satan was at that time ready with a trained angel awaiting the rise of those few wandering Grecian tribes into a vast and influential empire.
>
> —*The Prophecies of Daniel,* p. 308

There is an invisible warfare continually being waged around us. The goal is to influence the nations and governments to join Satan in his attempt to thwart the work of God and His ultimate victory. Paul sums it up in Ephesians 6:12: "For we wrestle not against flesh and blood, but against principalities, against powers, against the rulers of the darkness of this world, against spiritual wickedness in high places."

Ruling Angels

The next angels in the list of organization are those listed in Colossians 1:16. "For by him were all things created, that are in heaven, and that are in earth, visible and invisible, whether they be thrones, or dominions, or principalities, or powers: all things were created by him, and for him." These seem to be involved in ruling and listed in order of power, descending in rank from greatest to least.

Rulers or principalities are listed seven times by Paul in Romans 8:28; Ephesians 1:21, 3:10, 6:12; Colossians 1:16, 2:10, 15. Each of these indicate an order of angels, both good and evil, that are involved in governing the universe. Authorities and powers are listed in Ephesians 1:21, 2:2, 3:10; Colossians 1:16, 2:10,15; 1 Peter 3:22. They likely emphasize superhuman authority of angels and demons exercised in relation to the affairs of the world.

Powers are listed in 2 Peter 2:11; Ephesians 1:21; and 1 Peter 3:22. Powers relate to the fact that angels and demons have more power than man. Place of rule is mentioned only in Ephesians 6:12, where demons are designated as world rulers of darkness. Thrones or dominions are listed in Ephesians 1:21; Colossians 1:16; 2 Peter 2:10; and Jude 8. This emphasizes the dignity and authority of angelic rulers used in government.

Marvin R. Vincent states in *Word Studies in the New Testament* that thrones probably means enthroned angels. Dominions mean denominations. Principalities mean princedoms. Principalities and powers are used of both good and evil powers, but primarily refer to celestial beings.

Chafer states in *Systematic Theology, Vol. 2,* that these are governmental rulers specified as certain groups. There is a specific meaning for each group "which bear these appellations." The term "thrones" refers to those who sit upon these thrones. The term "dominions" refers to those who rule. The term "principalities" refers to those who govern. The term "powers" refers to those who exercise supremacy. The term "authorities" refers to those who are invested with imperial responsibility.

Although we have no indication in Scripture as to how many of these angels exist, we have an indication from Daniel 10 that all governments are assigned angels at every level. Governments represent order, because God established them to represent Him and maintain His order. God is in charge of governments: ". . . he removeth kings, and setteth up kings" (Dan. 2:21). Satan hates governments because they represent order, and he hates order.

God's plan to bring His creation full circle has never changed. His creation began in perfection and will finish and continue in perfection. Although the way God governs man changes, His ultimate plan and goal never changes. In other words, He doesn't use one plan until it fails, and then come up with another plan. The way He deals with the governing of man is by dispensations. According to the *Scofield Reference Bible,* "a dispensation is a period of time during which man is tested in respect of obedience to some *specific* revelation of the will of God. Seven such dispensations are distinguished in Scripture."

Each period is a time of stewardship in which man is provided a way to prove himself worthy of God's acceptance. Each succeeding dispensation is added to the last dispensation and swallowed up into the entire system. For instance, today we live in the dispensation of grace. The previous dispensation, law, was not eradicated; it was fulfilled by its succeeding dispensation, grace. So today we live in a dispensation that actually contains all preceding dispensations.

These seven dispensations will be discussed later. However, we will mention the dispensation of human government because of its relevance to this section. The dispensation of human government was established in Genesis 8:15–11:9. Noah was given a new stewardship within which to live. It included the things of the past plus new regulations. Now, the fear of man was placed upon the animals; man was allowed to eat animal flesh; he would never again live under the fear of a universal flood; and the institution of capital punishment was put into place. In essence, this gave man the right to govern others.

Immediately, Satan began to influence the steward of this new dispensation, Noah. Noah planted a vineyard, made wine, and got drunk. The fingerprint of Satan and his angels are found immediately. Therefore, Satan led the people away from God and followed his own law of rebellion. As a result, God scattered and confused the people, proving once again that humans in their fallen state are incapable of governing themselves.

For every plan of God for man, Satan has a counterplan. Satan and his angels are extremely active in the governments of man, and continually fight the holy angels so as to try and thwart the work of God. If man does not respect his God, he will not respect his government, but will attempt to replace it with some form of chaos.

Elect Angels

The "elect angels" are only mentioned once in the Bible: "I charge thee before God, and the Lord Jesus Christ, and the elect angels, that thou observe these things without preferring one before another, doing nothing by partiality" (1 Tim. 5:21). In this account the angels are said to witness what happens in the church. These elect angels are the holy angels. We might add that evil angels also witness church activities.

In *Systematic Theology, Vol. 2,* Chafer raises the question of sovereign election regarding the elect angels. Can this doctrine be extended to man? Angels were created for a purpose, and as for man "the designs of the Creator are to be executed to infinity." He points out that God was no more taken by surprise that the angels fell than He was by the fall of man. He adds that angels have now passed their probation. This does not mean that the fallen angels may experience forgiveness and grace, but that their destiny has been decided.

Certainly, we would agree that God was not unaware that the fall would take place, but did He intend for this to take place? We would have to say no. God created everything perfect, and to say that some were created to fall would be inconsistent with His attributes. The elect angels are those who remained holy and will continue to serve God throughout eternity.

Watchers and Holy Ones

The last angels to be considered are found in Daniel 4:13, 17, and 23. We read in verse 17:

> This matter is by the decree of the watchers, and the demand by the word of the holy ones: to the intent that the living may know that the most High ruleth in the kingdom of men, and giveth it to whomsoever he will, and setteth up over it the basest of men.

The identity of these angels is not clear, but is there is a difference between a "watcher" and a "holy one"? We know from verse 17 that there are more than one, but no exact number is given. In *The Prophecies of Daniel,* Strauss states of these angels, "these vigilant, sleepless creatures keep up an unceasing guard, functioning as agents of God's judgment." He further states that one of these angels is the "destroyer" that killed the firstborn of Egypt in Exodus 12:23. The *Ryrie Study Bible* and Fausset in *A Commentary, Vol. 2,* both indicate that the two are the same. The "angel that destroyed the people" also appears in 2 Samuel 24:16 and is directly under the authority of "the angel of the Lord."

The divine executioners of Ezekiel 9:1–7 may also be watchers. God is angry with the inhabitants of Jerusalem because of their abominations of idolatry and sends His angels to destroy them.

> He cried also in mine ears with a loud voice, saying, Cause them that have charge over the city to draw near, even every man with his destroying weapon in his hand. And, behold, six men came from the way of the higher gate, which lieth toward the north, and every man a slaughter weapon in his hand; and one man among them was clothed with linen, with a writer's inkhorn by his side: and they went in, and stood beside the brasen altar.
>
> —Ezekiel 9:1–2

This angel clothed with linen is described as the angel in Daniel 10 that was detained by the prince of Persia. Fausset is wrong in his assessment when he states:

> This same garment is assigned to the angel of the Lord (for which Michael is but another name) in the contemporary prophet Daniel (Daniel 10:5; 12:6–7). Therefore the Intercessory High Priest in heaven must be meant (Zechariah 1:12). The six with Him are His subordinates; therefore He is said to be "among them"—lit., "in the midst of them, as their recognized Lord" (Hebrews 1:6).
>
> —*A Commentary, Vol. 2,* p. 228

Although most disagree, these angels seem likely to be

two distinct and different beings. Both names appear in all three verses in Daniel (4:13, 17, 23) and are separated by the conjunction "and." In normal sentence structure, the conjunction "and" joins two separate items or personalities. In this case, the "watcher" carries the authority from God and the "holy one" enforces the message. This seems to be borne out in verse 17. The decree is by the watchers and the demand of the holy ones for the orders to be carried out "that the living may know that the most High ruleth in the kingdom of men."

In verse 23, a watcher and a holy one announce a decree. The order to "hew the tree down . . . yet leave the stump" is not an order to cut down a physical tree. Only an angel could accomplish this task, because the order was supernatural. Then to whom are they directing this order? One possible explanation is that the watcher was directing the holy one to carry out the command of God.

It is, however, difficult to be dogmatic with no more information than is given us. The only thing we can be certain of is that these were God's angels. There are many different organizations and types of angels, both holy and evil, and each type has a different task to accomplish, and their place in God's scheme of things. Even with all the information we are given in Scripture, we remain in the dark and uncertain about certain of these spirit beings. God gives us the knowledge on the basis of a "need to know," and someday we will know all.

Chapter Five

The Ministry of Angels in the Old Testament

We have already established that God works with man in a period of time (or of testing) called a dispensation. There are seven dispensations or times of testing for man in the entire Bible. In the Old Testament the dispensations are listed as the dispensations of innocence, conscience, human government, promise, and law, as taught in Scofield's notes. Although these may not seem to be adequate in some ways, they are still the best that have been offered. In each of these dispensations the angels were very active, both holy and evil.

The Dispensation of Innocence

The dispensation of innocence began with the creation of Adam and ended with his fall. It is recorded in Genesis 1:28–3:6. This is the shortest of all the recorded dispensations, probably because it did not take man long to sin. As Ryrie points out, innocence may not exactly give us the correct view of Adam.

> Although this term is not a good description of Adam's condition before the Fall, it may be the best single word. Yet the word *innocent* seems too neutral. Adam was not created merely innocent but with a positive holiness that enabled him to have face-to-face communication with God.
>
> —Charles Ryrie, *Dispensationalism,* p. 51

Adam was sinless and complete, but had never experienced a choice of obedience or disobedience. Adam was created dependent on God, and with his disobedience came independence from God. He decided in his heart that he could get along without God's help. He wanted to do it himself. His innocence was put to the test when offered an option by the only angel we see in the garden. That angel was Satan disguised as a serpent, an animal that Adam had shared the garden with since creation.

Adam's only employment was to dress and keep the garden, and his only restriction was not to eat of one fruit. He could have anything in the garden he wanted to eat except the fruit of "the tree of knowledge of good and evil." Here Satan offered to them the possibility of becoming "as gods." They ate of the fruit and joined Satan in the same folly that he himself had aspirations of becoming, as God. This is the only recorded activity of angels during this dispensation.

The Dispensation of Conscience

The second period is the dispensation of conscience. This period is recorded in Genesis 4:1–8:14 and extends from

Adam's fall to the flood. After the fall, Adam and Eve were ejected from the garden and no longer had God's fellowship as in the pristine state. They then had to rely on their memory of what was correct and good, their conscience. The conscience is the capability of the human soul to pass moral judgment on its own thoughts and actions. They were created with a perfect conscience and had to rely on that memory of right and wrong. Their sons and daughters were born with a conscience that was corrupted by the fall but still knew that God existed. Paul states in Romans 1:19 that even today man is born with an innate knowledge that He exists. "Because that which may be known of God is manifest in them; for God hath shewed it unto them." Only when they have been exposed to the truth of the gospel can that conscience be righted.

In Genesis this dispensation is opened with angelic activity in the form of cherubims guarding the gate to Eden (3:24). Abel responded to his conscience by offering a blood sacrifice to please God (4:4). As Abel pleased God, Cain displeased God and disregarded his conscience by offering from "the fruit of the ground" at the possible prompting of Satan (4:3, 5). Jealousy reared its ugly head and the first murder followed (4:8). The stench of the activity of Satan and his evil angels reek in the wickedness of every thought and action of man (6:5). Angels cohabited with women and produced giants that were half human and half angels (6:4). Violence and corruption became the rule, and God sent a universal flood to destroy His creation as well as the universal wickedness (6:7).

The Dispensation of Human Government

This third period is the dispensation of human government. This period is recorded in Genesis 8:15–11:9 and extends from the flood to the call of Abraham. As discussed earlier, Noah was the steward that God placed in charge of this stewardship. Noah went forth from the ark and promptly built an altar and sacrificed one of every clean beast and God was pleased (8:20). God then made a covenant with Noah that the earth would never again be destroyed by flood (8:21). The flesh of animals was added to the diet and the fear of man was placed on all animal life (9:2–3). And capital punishment was given to enforce the power to rule (9:5–6).

However, Noah failed to properly govern. Almost immediately he planted a vineyard, made wine, and became drunk (9:20–21). As a result of his drunkenness, his son Ham saw his father in his nakedness and reported it to his brothers Shem and Japheth (9:22). Some believe that Ham ridiculed his father instead of covering him. Because of Ham's actions, Noah cursed his son to become a "servant of servants" to his brothers (9:25–26).

Satan and his angels surely were at work to salvage their world and retain rule over these humans. In chapters ten and eleven, under the leadership of Nimrod, a descendent of Ham, Satan once again pulled man together to try to complete his rebellion against God. All the people of the earth lived at one place and spoke one language. They tried to build a tower that would reach into heaven. Satan once again attempted to exalt his throne above the stars of God (Isa. 14:12–15). Again he was doomed to failure; all the people were scattered and their language was confounded so that they could no longer communicate (Gen. 11:5–9).

Although we cannot see Satan and his angels at work, we can see their footprints everywhere with their exit from the ark to the tower of Babel. Satan was attempting to raise up a universal ruler in Nimrod and establish a world empire. The only place that Noah and his family found any solace was in the ark itself. God again proved gracious because He did not utterly destroy the people, but immediately turned to His friend, Abram.

The Dispensation of Promise

The dispensation of promise is recorded in Genesis 11:10–Exodus 18:27 and extends from the call of Abraham to the giving and acceptance of the Mosiac Law at Sinai. This dispensation gets its name from Hebrews 11:9: "By faith he sojourned in the land of promise, as in a strange country, dwelling in tabernacles with Isaac and Jacob, the heirs with him of the same promise."

"Until this dispensation, all mankind had been directly related to God's governing principles. Now God marked out one family and one nation and in them made a representative test of all" (*Dispensationalism,* p. 51).

In this dispensation, the angel that is most mentioned is the angel of the Lord, which we have covered extensively in a previous chapter. We have also adequately discussed the two angels that went to the aid of Lot in Genesis 19.

The next angels mentioned are the angels associated with Jacob's dream in Genesis 28:10. In verse 12 we read of these angels: "And he dreamed, and behold a ladder set up on the earth, and the top of it reached to heaven: and behold the angels of God ascending and descending on it." The angel's activity and presence here is unclear. In volume 1 of *A Commentary,* Robert Jamieson states that "the angels were continually ascending and descending from God Himself on their benevolent errands."

Keil says, concerning the ladder and the angels:

> After making a pillow with the stones, he fell asleep and had a dream, in which he saw a ladder resting upon the earth, with the top reaching to heaven; and upon it angels of God going up and down, and Jehovah Himself standing above it. The ladder was a visible symbol of the real and uninterrupted fellowship between God in heaven and His people upon the earth. The angels upon it carry up the wants of men to God, and bring down the assistance and protection of God to men. The ladder stood there upon the earth, just where Jacob was lying in solitude, poor, helpless, and forsaken by men.... The revelation was intended not only to stamp the blessing, with which Isaac had dismissed him from his home, with the seal of divine approval, but to impress upon Jacob's mind the fact, that although Jehovah would be near to protect and guide him even in a foreign land, the land of promise was the holy ground on which the God of his fathers would set up the covenant of His grace.
>
> —*Commentary on the Old Testament, Vol. 1,* p. 281

Ryle states:

> An evident allusion to Jacob's vision is found in

> Christ's words recorded in Jn. 1:51. The ladder or stairway is shown by this statement to represent Jesus Christ Himself, the One who connects heaven and earth. "When He comes the second time to take His great power and reign, the words of this text shall be literally fulfilled."
>
> —*Wycliffe's Bible Encyclopedia, Vol. 2,* p. 1003

Edersheim also connects this passage to John 1:51, that the ladder is none other than Jesus Christ. He states:

> And what Jacob heard, that he also saw in symbolic vision. The *promise* was the real God-built stair, which reached from the lonely place on which the poor wanderer lay quite up to heaven. . . . Below lies poor, helpless, forsaken man; above, stands Jehovah Himself, and upon the ladder of promise which joins earth to heaven, the angels of God, in their silent, never-ceasing ministry, descend, bringing help, and ascend, as to fetch new deliverance. Nay, this "ladder" is Christ, for by this "ladder" God Himself has come down to us in the Person of His dear Son, Who is, so to speak, the Promise become Reality, as it is written: "Hereafter ye shall see heaven open, and the angels of God ascending and descending upon the Son of Man" (John 1:51).
>
> —*Bible History, Old Testament,* p. 87

All seem to agree that the ministry of the angels here is to attend to the needs of God's people, and the conduit between God and man is none other than Jesus Christ.

It is also shown that the angels are the method of transporting these blessings and assurances from the Father to man through Jesus Christ. "Are they not all ministering spirits, sent forth to minister for them who shall be heirs of salvation?" (Heb. 1:14).

In Genesis 31, we see the next appearance of an angel. In verse 11 we read: "And the angel of God spake unto me in a dream, saying, Jacob: And I said, Here am I." We know that this is no ordinary angel because of what we read in verse 13, which are the comments of the angel. "I am the God of Beth-el, where thou anointedst the pillar, and where thou vowedst a vow unto me: now arise, get thee out from this land, and return unto the land of thy kindred." This is the same as the angel of the Lord in other passages and has been previously covered, the pre-incarnate Son of God. However, in Genesis 32:1 we read of plural "angels of God": "And Jacob went on his way, and the angels of God met him." The plurality of these angels of God precludes any identity as the pre-incarnate Son of God. They are simply identified as holy angels in verse 2, "This is God's host."

The last time the word angel appears in the dispensation of promise is in Genesis 48:16: "The Angel which redeemed me from all evil, bless the lads; and let my name be named on them, and the name of my fathers Abraham and Isaac; and let them grow into a multitude in the midst of the earth." Here Israel is blessing Joseph and his two sons, Manasseh and Ephraim. The Angel in verse 16 is referring back to the God of verse 15, and is no ordinary angel. The "God which fed me all my life long unto this day" (God my Shepherd) is the Angel of verse 16. In verse 16 we see the first time in the Bible where the term "redeemed" is used. It means "to save" or "to be a savior or deliverer."

Of this passage Edersheim writes: "In this threefold reference to God as the convenant-God, the Shepherd, and the Angel-Redeemer, we have a distinct anticipation of the truth concerning the blessed Trinity" (*Bible History*, p. 87).

Keil echoes the same conclusion:

> This triple reference to God, in which the Angel who is placed on an equality with *Ha-Elohim* cannot possibly be a created angel, but must be the "Angel of God," *i.e.* God manifested in the form of the Angel of Jehovah, or the "Angel of His face" (Isa.43:9), contains a foreshadowing of the Trinity, though only God and the Angel are distinguished, not three persons of the divine nature.
>
> —*Commentary on the Old Testament, Vol. 1,* p. 383

The angelic activity in this dispensation is limited in its places of mention. That both holy and evil angels were active is certain, but the mention of them is few. However, the incidences of angelic activity in the dispensation of law greatly increases above that of any other dispensation.

The Dispensation of Law

The dispensation of law is recorded in Scripture from Exodus 19:1 to Acts 1, or from the giving of the Mosaic

Law to the death of Christ. Under this economy, the people were responsible to keep the Law (Jam. 2:10). They failed miserably (Rom. 10:1–3). Because of their failure, there was a continual long period of judgments. We are told in Romans 3:20 that the Law was not a means of justification, but of condemnation.

The scriptural recording of angelic activity during this period greatly increases. For the first time man is responsible to a written code, and his morality is measured by it. It is now that Satan can surely accuse the saints on grounds that they know better. Until now man has been responsible to God under direct communication or through the governing of other men. It is now written in stone and they are without excuse. Paul states in Romans 4:15: "Because the law worketh wrath: for where no law is, there is no transgression." The Law does not cause wrath; it simply points it out when it has been violated.

In this section, we will only discuss unexplored major angelic activity through the end of the Old Testament, not to the end of the Law. The vast majority of angelic activity in the dispensation of law is by the "angel of the Lord." There are only a few remaining cases that continue to be unexplored.

In Daniel 12, the angel warned Daniel that the Tribulation would be a time of unprecedented suffering. In verse 5 the angel says: "Then I Daniel looked, and, behold, there stood other two, the one on this side of the bank of the river, and the other on that side of the bank of the river." These two were most likely angels. It could also be suggested that these two men in verse 5 could be the "two witnesses" of Revelation 11. They appear in both places as the Great Tribulation is about to begin. The one that is clothed in linen and is upon the river is the same angel that Daniel saw in chapter 10. This is sure to be the angel of the Lord.

The book of Zechariah mentions the word "angels" twenty times, of which six are the angel of the Lord. Here in this book is a message of hope and a call to repentance. Zechariah has a total of eight visions that he has all in one night. In 1:8 he sees his first vision and it concerns a man riding a red horse. The angel in verse 9 is not the same angel of verse 8. The angel that rode the red horse is the angel of the Lord. The angel of the Lord proceeds to tell Zechariah that the Gentile nations were flourishing and secure, and Israel was still downtrodden. The Temple has lain in ruins for seventy years, and the Lord of Hosts will certainly remember Israel in her time of trouble.

In 1:19–20 he receives the vision of the four horns and the four carpenters. The angel of the Lord tells him of the four Gentile nations that have afflicted and scattered Israel (vs. 21). These nations were represented by four horns representing four powers. These four horns are also called carpenters. In 2:1–2 he receives the vision of the surveyor. The angels speak of the assured restoration of Israel and Jerusalem. The angels tell Zechariah that in the future millennium Jerusalem will extend beyond its walls.

In 3:1 he receives the vision of the high priest. Joshua, the high priest, was standing before the angel of the Lord, and Satan stood "at his right hand to resist him." The Lord rebukes Satan and states that Israel has been saved from the fire of Babylon's captivity and is "a brand plucked out of the fire." In verse 7 the Lord told Zechariah that if he would "walk in my ways, and if thou wilt keep my charge, then thou shalt also judge my house, and shalt also keep my courts, and I will give thee places to walk among these that stand by." Those that stood by were angels. He would be able to walk with angels.

In chapter four Zechariah receives the vision of the golden candlestick from the angel of the Lord. Each candlestick had seven lamps and seven pipes to each lamp for a total of forty-nine conduits in all. The angel then showed him the two olive trees, one standing on each side of the bowl. These represent the kingly and priestly offices of Zerubbabel and Joshua. In verse 14 they are called the "two anointed ones," possibly referring to the two witness of Revelation 11.

In chapter five he receives the vision of the flying roll and the vision of the woman in the ephah from the angel. In verses 1–4 the flying roll represents God's judgment against sinners. In verses 5-11 the woman in the ephah represents wickedness and is banished to Shinar (Babylon). The two women with wings that come out of the ephah are not angels. They have the wings of storks, and therefore must represent forces of evil.

In chapter six he receives the vision of the four chariots. The first chariot was pulled by red horses; the second by black horses; the third by white horses; and the fourth by grisled and bay horses. This is a vision of God's judgment on the nations of the world. The chariots all go in different directions and are instruments of Divine judgments. These "spirits of the heavens" may be angels of judgment. The "spirit" here means anger.

The last mention of the angel of the Lord, as well as the term "angel" in the Old Testament appears in Zechariah 12:8: "In that day shall the LORD defend the inhabitants of Jerusalem; and he that is feeble among them at that day shall be as David; and the house of David shall be as God, as the angel of the LORD before them." Even the most feeble Jerusalemite will be empowered to fight like David, and the leaders will be as powerful as God.

The Old Testament ends with the book of Malachi, and no notice of angelic activity. This book is a book of warning, as well as hope, looking forward to Christ's kingdom. The Jews have declined in their zeal to serve the Lord and are guilty of scorn and contempt. Since finishing the Temple, they have cooled in their love for God and His work. The work of Satan is evident, and the people are guilty of robbing God. Because of their attitude toward the Lord, He will not directly speak to the chief priest for four hundred years, hence the four hundred silent years. During this time Israel will be a battleground for opposing armies, and the antichrist of the Old Testament is introduced, Antiochus Epiphanes.

Satan and his angels are very active during this period, and seem to rule Israel and the world until the announcement of the Savior in Matthew. With the announcement of the Savior, angelic activity again begins to accelerate. The closing of the Old Testament does not bring an end to the Law. It must continue on into the New Testament until the death of Christ.

Chapter Six

The Ministry of Angels in the New Testament

The Ministry of the Angels During the Gospels

Introduction. The New Testament opens with the Gospels and the continuation of the dispensation of law. Israel had experienced great hardships during the last four hundred years under Persian, Greek, Ptolemy, and finally Roman rule. In 198 B.C. after the Ptolemies had ruled about a hundred years, the Syrians under the leadership of Antiochus III took Syria and Palestine away from Egypt. These Syrians were known as Seleucids.

When strife between the Hellenizers and the Jews broke out over the priesthood, Antiochus IV, the Seleucid who succeeded Antiochus III, aligned himself against the Jews. Antiochus IV was known as Antiochus Epiphanes, a self-appointed title meaning "illustrious one." He marched on Jerusalem and consequently killed seventy thousand Jews and took another seventy thousand captive. He also plundered the Temple and took the Temple utensils and treasures back to Syria. He then offered a sow on the altar and forbade the continuation of daily sacrifices, after which he burned the Scriptures and forced the Jews to eat swine's flesh.

The Jews responded by forming their own army under the leadership of an aged priest, Mattathias. Mattathias and his guerrilla army fled to the mountains and used them as headquarters from which to wage war against Epiphanes and his Syrian army. After the death of Mattathias, his son Judas, surnamed Maccabee, took over the leadership and regained possession of Jerusalem by 164 B.C. Under his leadership he purified the Temple and began the daily sacrifice once again. Soon after losing Jerusalem to the "Maccabees," Epiphanes died, but the war continued for another twenty years.

In subsequent years the threat of civil war entered the Maccabbean rule which forced Rome into Jerusalem. Upon arriving at Jerusalem, the Roman general Pompey entered the Holy of Holies but, unlike Epiphanes, he did not touch the Temple treasures. Under Mark Antony, Herod was placed into office as king of the Jews. The Herodians believed that it was best for Judaism to cooperate with Rome religiously as well as politically. This religious and political oppression by Rome set the stage for the birth of Christ.

When Christ was born in Bethlehem, there were several political and religious self-interest groups that demanded their own needs be fulfilled. The Pharisees were a religious group of pious Jews known as "separatists." These were a strict fundamentalist group filled with pride and hypocrisy. They believed in the resurrection, but were denounced by Jesus as hypocrites. Paul was a member of this group. They controlled the synagogues.

The Sadducees were probably named for Zadok, the high priest appointed by Solomon (1 Kings 2:35). They strictly followed the Law of Moses and did not like tradition. They denied the doctrines of resurrection, angels, and the existence of spirits. They were mainly people of wealth and position, and they controlled the priesthood and Temple ritual.

The Essenes were both religious and political. They were hermits that exercised self-denial and celibacy. They removed themselves from society and were given to Scripture reading, prayer, and ceremonial cleansings, and were very industrious. The caves near where the Dead Sea Scrolls were found are thought to be the Essene center in the Judean wilderness.

The scribes were not a sect but a profession. They were regarded as the authority on the Scriptures and spent their lives copying the Law. Their thinking was more in line with the Pharisees than any other group.

These were the religious conditions into which our Lord was born. There was hatred and suspicion among all the religious sects, and each one demanded something different in the soon-coming Messiah. He would be rejected or accepted depending on the message He preached both politically and religiously. The same conditions exist today. His soon return is awaited with different expectations by many groups that call themselves Christians.

Angels in the Gospels. The "angel of the Lord" has been extensively considered previously, and we will not belabor the point as to His identity in the Gospels except to say that it is the same as in the Old Testament. The angel of the Lord is the Second Person of the Trinity and remains so until the incarnation of Jesus. He is mentioned on several occasions in the Gospels and it can be stated that He announced His own birth. In some instances, such as Matthew 2:19, the incarnation has already taken place, and the term is "an angel of the Lord." The indefinite article "an" is used instead of the definite article "the," meaning that the angel is simply a messenger.

Angels were active in every phase of the announcement and birth of Christ. They attended Him before birth and ministered to Him as a young child. In Matthew 2:13 we read how an angel warned Joseph in a dream:

> And when they were departed, behold, *the* angel of the Lord appeareth to Joseph in a dream, saying, Arise, and take the young child and his mother, and flee into Egypt, and be thou there until I bring thee word: for Herod will seek the young child to destroy him.

The holy angels attended Christ in the garden (Matt. 26:53), at the cross, at His resurrection (Matt. 28:2), and at His ascension (Acts 1:10).

The term "the angel of the Lord" should have been translated "an angel of the Lord." The Greek definite article does not appear in the original text. The original Koine Greek does not contain words for indefinite articles, only definite articles. These indefinite articles were added by the King James translators to make the reading easier.

This is not being disrespectful of the King James Version (I use no other), it is merely an oversight by the translators. We believe that the King James Version is the preserved English text, but the writings in the original Hebrew and Greek are the inspired text. The point is that the angel sent by God knew beforehand what Satan and his angels were planning for the young Jesus. The sides had been chosen and the battle plan was being drawn up by Satan to try to destroy the Child and eliminate the Savior of the world.

The main message of the Gospels is the offering of the kingdom of heaven or the Millennium. This we see is a valid offer, but it is rejected by the Jews by their proclaiming, "We'll not have this man to rule over us." The offer of the gospel of the kingdom of heaven was met with stiff resistance by Satan and the fallen angels (called demons in the Gospels). If Jesus had been accepted by the nation of Israel at this time, the Millennium would have been ushered in.

The term "demon" is always translated "devil" in the King James Version of the Bible. The Greek term for "demon" is *diamonion,* while the Greek term for "devil" is *diabolos.* Unless the term is capitalized or preceded by the definite article "the," it is a demon or fallen angel.

Most cases of angelic activity in the Gospels were in the form of demon possession. In many cases Jesus used this possession as a sign of His power over Satan, and as proof of His deity by casting out these demons from their host. These demons are highly organized and have a leader. This leader is none other than Satan himself, and we will discuss him first.

Satan. Satan is called the adversary, the devil, and the slanderer. His existence is taught in seven of the Old Testament books and by every New Testament author. He is a murderer and a liar (John 8:44); he is forever a sinner (1 John 3:8); he is an accuser (Rev. 12:10); and he is an adversary (1 Pet. 5:8). He is the leader of the demons and continually enlists their aid in his quest to defeat the Lord. In the Gospels, as the kingdom of heaven is offered, Satan has but one goal: to eliminate the possibility of this kingdom. In order to accomplish this he must kill the King, for without a King there can be no kingdom. Though it is not stated, it is implied that Satan was behind the plan to kill all male babies in Israel to be sure that they eliminated the one represented by the prophecy (Matt. 2:16). He believed that he had accomplished this with Christ's death on the cross (Matt. 27:45; Mark 15:33–41; Luke 23:44–49; John 19:30–37).

The first time we see him by name in the Gospels is in Matthew 4:1: "Then was Jesus led up of the Spirit into the wilderness to be tempted of the devil." "Then" would mean that immediately after His baptism, He was led up out of the Jordan Valley to some elevated spot.

In *Studies of the Four Gospels* G. Campbell Morgan states that the King had not come merely to reign, but He must first subdue the kingdom to Himself. Before He can receive the kingdom and reign over it, He must demonstrate that He is personally victorious over the forces of antagonism by defeating the foe. He has been attested to as being perfect in harmony, and now He must face the disorder and ugliness of the abyss. Matthew reveals Him to us in three ways: as a perfect man; a man demonstrated perfect through testing; and as a man victorious and fitted for supremacy.

In volume 3 of *A Commentary,* Brown relates that the Spirit led Him into the wilderness simply to have his faith tried, and the agent was the wicked one, Satan. He adds that the word used here is *diabolos,* signifying a slanderer or one who casts imputations upon another. In Mark 1:13 He was for forty days tempted by Satan. Here the word used is a word signifying an *adversary.* These and other names of the same fallen spirit are used of different features in his character or actions.

This is all by design, Brown states. First, to give our Lord a taste of what lay before Him. Second, to make trial of the glorious and necessary equipment He had just received. Last, to encourage Him through the victory He is about to experience, and going forward spoiling principalities and powers until triumphing over them on His cross.

We must disagree with Brown in his conclusions, based on the deity and therefore the omniscience of the God-man, Jesus. His experience of suffering was not for Himself, for He was already sinless and needed not to suffer. His suffering was to experience every pain man was to suffer and prove His deity, for no one less than God could have endured and triumphed over Satan. However, we must agree with Morgan, as stated previously, that Jesus needed to subdue Satan's kingdom and defeat him before moving to set up His own kingdom.

Willmington states that Jesus passed the temptation test, resisted Satan, and showed Himself qualified as the spotless Lamb of God to be the perfect sacrifice.

By refusing to satisfy his hunger by turning the stones

> into bread, he conquered the lust for physical pleasure. By rejecting Satan's dare to jump from the top of the Temple, he conquered pride in one's possessions. By turning down Satan's offer of the kingdoms of the world, he conquered the lust of everything one sees.
>
> —*Bible Handbook,* p. 526

Satan's method that was used against Jesus was the same that was used in the garden of Eden against Adam and Eve. In Genesis 3 the serpent tempted Eve to eat of the forbidden fruit by using the same tactics. We see her response in verse 6:

> And when the woman saw that the tree was good for food, and that it was pleasant to the eyes, and a tree to be desired to make one wise, she took of the fruit thereof, and did eat, and gave also unto her husband with her; and he did eat.

Where Satan was successful in the garden, he was unsuccessful in the wilderness. John echoes Satan's tactics in 1 John 2:16: "For all that is in the world, the lust of the flesh, and the lust of the eyes, and the pride of life, is not of the Father, but is of the world."

In *Matthew—Thy Kingdom Come,* Walvoord relates that Satan followed the exact same plan that he followed when he tempted Eve. The first temptation appeals to the lust of the flesh; it was good for food. Satan told Jesus that if He were the Son of God He could turn the stones to bread to satisfy His hunger. Jesus countered by referring to Deuteronomy 8:3: "It is written, Man shall not live by bread alone, but by every word that proceedeth out of the mouth of God" (Matt. 4:4). The second temptation appeals to the lust of the eyes; it was pleasant to the eyes. Satan told Jesus that if He were the Son of God He could jump from the pinnacle of the Temple and the angels would catch Him. Jesus answered by referring to Deuteronomy 6:16: "It is written again, Thou shalt not tempt the Lord thy God" (vs. 7). The third temptation appeals to the pride of life; it appeals to the ego. Jesus answered by referring to Deuteronomy 6:13 and 10:20.

Unger points out:

> Doubtless, very crucial cases of temptations (Matt. 4:1; Luke 22:3; 22:31) are the direct task of Satan himself, but since he is neither omnipresent, nor omnipotent, nor omniscient, the greater part of this colossal activity must be thought of as delegated to demons.
>
> —*Biblical Demonology,* p. 69

When Satan had expended all his temptations, he left Jesus and the "angels came and ministered unto him" (4:11).

Beelzebub. "Further revelation concerning Satan presents him as a king with a kingdom (Matt. 12:26), a portion of which dominion consists of demons (Matt. 12:24)" (*Biblical Demonology,* p. 15). In the Gospels another demon is known by the name Beelzebub (Matt. 12:24), "prince of the devils." This name is thought to be another name for Satan by some, and not, by others. *Smith's Bible Dictionary* states that this actually should be translated "Beelzebul" and not "Beelzebub," but agrees that this is the title of a heathen deity that the Jews ascribed to the "sovereignty of the evil spirits" that is Satan, the prince of the demons.

Willmington states that "Beelzebub" comes from a Canaanite deity and was a common name for Satan.

> Baal is Canaanite for "lord." One of Baal's names was "Baal-zebul," which means "lord of the height," signifying his supremacy. The Israelites tried to mock Baal by changing this to the similar-sounding "Baal-zebub" (1:2), which means "lord of the flies" and suggests that Baal is really lord of nothing. The derogatory name would later be used to describe Satan.
>
> —*Bible Handbook,* p. 209

Payne agrees that this name designates Satan as the "chief of the devils." However, he adds:

> No definite connection can be made between Baalzebub (2 Kgs 1:2, "lord of flies") and the NT *Beelzeboul.* Alternative doubtful derivations include *Ba'al zebul,* "lord of the dwelling" (cf. Mt 10:25; '"they have called the *master of the house* Beelzebul"), or "lord of dung" (2 Kgs 1:2; the Philistine deity Baalzebul mocked as Baalzebub, "lord of flies").
>
> —*Wycliffe Bible Encyclopedia, Vol. 1,* p. 212

Even though the *Textus Receptus* spells the name in question, *Beelzeboul,* it is agreed by most scholars that the one called by the name of Beelzebub in the King James Version is truly Satan, the prince of the demons. Jesus Himself settles the question with His answer in verse 26: "And if Satan cast out Satan, he is divided against himself; how shall then his kingdom stand?" Certainly he is referring to Beelzebub and the demons in the statement by the Pharisees in verse 24: "This fellow doth not cast out devils, but by Beelzebub the prince of the devils." Satan by any other name is still Satan.

The point that Jesus is making is that Satan cannot and will not cast himself out of his own place (12:25). If Satan cannot, then someone else must be casting Satan out of his place. The only one that is capable of doing this is God, and if God is performing this, then the kingdom of God has come to them in the form of the Son (12:28).

Angel at the Pool of Bethesda. In John 5:4 we read in the King James Version of a peculiar thing that happened at the pool of Bethesda. "For an angel went down at a certain season into the pool, and troubled the water: whosoever then first after the troubling of the water stepped in was made whole of whatsoever disease he had." Some have questioned the authenticity of this verse and have said that it should be left out. Many of the new translations based on the Westcott and Hort text, such as the NIV and ASV, leave this verse out with the typical explanation that "some less important manuscripts" contain this verse. Of course, the less important manuscript mentioned must be the *Textus Receptus,* because it contains this verse.

The *Wycliffe Bible Commentary* states that these verses are a part of tradition of the early church which, I might add, are normally based on fact.

> The five porches or porticoes, now uncovered, sheltered a great company of sick, some **blind,** others **lame,** others **withered,** i.e., paralyzed. They were there in hope of being healed when the water was troubled. While our manuscript tradition is such that the end of verse 3 and all of verse 4 cannot be regarded as part of the original text of John, this portion is an early tradition. J. Rendel Harris found evidence in several places throughout the East of a superstition to the effect that at the New Year an angel was expected to stir the water in certain localities, enabling one person to obtain healing by being the first to get into the water after the disturbance. On this basis he judged the feast of this chapter to have been Trumpets, announcing the New Year (so [sic] Westcott. See J. Rendel Harris, *Side Lights on the New Testament Research,* pp. 36–69). The remains of the Church of St. Anne include the figure of an angel, testifying to this belief and the custom of seeking healing under these special circumstances.
>
> —*Wycliffe Bible Commentary,* p. 1082

Edward Hill states in *Believing Bible Study* that certain church fathers attached a great theological significance to the angel in John 5:4. These men regarded this as some type of baptism, and the angel as a type of precursor of the Holy Spirit. Tertullian, Didymus, Chrysostom, and Tatian all believed in the genuineness of the verse and believe that it is part of the canon. They believed that the angel is a forerunner of the Holy Spirit.

The manuscript tradition to disregard verse 4 is espoused by Westcott and Hort as a less important manuscript. They also espouse to add, change, or omit other passages, many of which are essential to the saving of our souls. There may be a manuscript found that has left out John 3:16. Can we then expect this verse to be omitted? John had firsthand knowledge of the facts and wrote them as instructed by the Holy Spirit. This should not be changed by the whim of those some eighteen hundred years removed, and adhered to by their followers all in the cause of academia. The truth has never been popular, but altering the text will not change the facts or the responsibility of those who accept those changes. For those who allow someone else to be their conscience, Paul wrote Romans 14:12: "So then every one of us shall give account of himself to God."

The word used for "angel" is the same word used throughout the New Testament. These translations leave out the fourth verse, omitting the number four in its chronological order, skipping from three to five. Why leave out the number four if the verse does not exist? In verse 3 we have sick folks waiting for something to happen. These people were waiting for the moving of the water, not an angel. Whether or not they knew the moving of the water was caused by an angel is not known, but certainly John did.

The fourth verse is necessary to explain and understand verse 7. "The impotent man answered him, Sir, I have no man, when the water is troubled, to put me into the pool: but while I am coming, another steppeth down before me." Jesus never questions the "troubling"; He heals the man and tells him, "Rise, take up thy bed, and walk." Without the fourth verse, there would be no continuity between third and seventh verse. The identity of the angel is not known, but we do know that angelic activity was involved.

The Unpardonable Sin. This accusation in itself has serious consequences, attributing the work of the Holy Spirit to Satan.

> Wherefore I say unto you, All manner of sin and blasphemy shall be forgiven unto men: but the blasphemy against the Holy Ghost shall not be forgiven unto men. And whosoever speaketh a word against the Son of man, it shall be forgiven him: but whosoever speaketh against the Holy Ghost, it shall not be forgiven him, neither in this world, neither in the world to come.
>
> —Matthew 12:31–32

Satan and his demons were involved in the dialogue concerning the "unpardonable sin" (Matt. 12:31–32; Mark 3:22–30; Luke 11: 14–23). What is the unpardonable sin, and can a person today commit the unpardonable sin? It is not clear if the scenario for Matthew would need to be reconstructed. Jesus was present, and He had just performed a miracle by casting out the demons, and the work of the Holy Spirit was attributed to Satan. Those conditions cannot be re-enacted today. We must also consider that these conditions were present under the dispensation of law, and we now live under the dispensation of grace.

Walvoord sums it up with this statement:

> There has been much misunderstanding about blasphemy against the Holy Spirit. Here it is properly defined as attributing to Satan what is accomplished by the power of God. Such a sin is not unpardonable in itself, but rather because it rejects the person and work of the Holy Spirit, without whom repentance and restoration are impossible. As far as it applies today, it is not the thought that one seeking pardon will not find it, but rather that one who rejects the Holy Spirit will not seek pardon.
>
> —*Matthew: Thy Kingdom Come,* p. 89

There is only one sin that can be committed today that will condemn one to hell: rejection of Jesus Christ as the Savior. This act in itself is rejecting the convicting ministry of the Holy Spirit.

Parable of the Sower. There are other instances of Satan's activity in the Gospels. In the parable of the sower (Matt. 13; Mark 4; Luke 8), Satan is said to be very influential and deceptive in dealing with the gospel of the kingdom. He immediately comes and steals the Word from those who do not comprehend it. In Matthew 13:24–28 Satan plants his followers among the true believers and they cannot be told apart. The servants came to the householder and asked him how to tell the difference between the wheat and tares. The householder warned them that to remove the tares would also uproot the wheat. They were told to wait until the harvest (resurrection) and the reapers (angels) would separate them and burn them (hell). The wheat (believers) would be gathered into the barn (heaven) (Matt. 13:36–43).

Peter Used of Satan. In Mark 8:32–33 Peter is used of Satan to try to persuade Jesus not to go to the cross.

> And he spake that saying openly. And Peter took him, and began to rebuke him. But when he had turned about and looked on his disciples, he rebuked Peter, saying, Get thee behind me, Satan: for thou savourest not the things that be of God, but the things that be of men.

Walvoord states in *Matthew: Thy Kingdom Come*: "The problem here was lack of spiritual discernment so common to man but not in keeping with Peter's place of leadership among the disciples." It is apparent that when Christ looked on His disciples after Peter's rebuke, He saw a question and concern in them also. Or, perhaps He saw something no one else saw, the presence of Satan himself.

In a narrative found only in Luke 10 we find an event that would make most pastors jealous: seventy out on visitation. Jesus must have had a large following at this time. In verse 17 the seventy came back to Him after a successful mission and reported that even the devils (demons) were subject to them through His name. To this He replied: "I beheld Satan as lightning fall from heaven" (vs. 18). The *Ryrie Study Bible* relates that the power of Satan was broken and the success of the seventy over Satan was proof of it. Jesus must certainly be looking forward to the cross (John 12:31, 16:11; Rev. 9:1, 12:8–9).

Judas Iscariot. In John 13 and Luke 22 we see Satan go beyond influencing an individual to possessing him. This Satan did twice to Judas. The first time was in Luke 22:3–4: "Then entered Satan into Judas surnamed Iscariot, being of the number of the twelve. And he went his way, and communed with the chief priests and captains, how he might betray him unto them."

The second time was in John 13:26–27 as Jesus was identifying the one who would betray Him.

> Jesus answered, He it is, to whom I shall give a sop, when I have dipped it. And when he had dipped the sop, he gave it to Judas Iscariot, the son of Simon. And after the sop Satan entered into him. Then said Jesus unto him, That thou doest, do quickly.

Morgan writes that this was Satan's final approach in attempting to reach Jesus, not by seductions as he did in the wilderness, but by a definite attack upon Him. He hoped to reach Him through a disciple and get Him in his power for death. Even he did not understand the significance of His dying. Satan won on a human level by gaining access to Judas and bringing about His betrayal, and to put Jesus on the cross. However, he found that his apparent victory of Christ's death was the hour in which the woman's seed bruised the serpent's head. Morgan states:

> I do not believe Judas was a man as other men. I believe he was a devil incarnate; I believe he was the son of perdition; and I believe that after his death, by

> his own hand, he went "to his own place." My own conviction has long been that Judas was raised up to do the darkest deed in human history, and that he was actually a devil incarnate.
>
> —*Studies in the Four Gospels,* p. 235

The fact that it was necessary for Satan to enter Judas on two different occasions was because he is not omnipresent. He could not carry on his normal duties and remain in Christ's presence by remaining in possession of Judas.

The "son of perdition" is referred to in Acts 1:20, as being a fulfillment of Psalm 109:6–8: "Set thou a wicked man over him: and let Satan stand at his right hand. When he shall be judged, let him be condemned: and let his prayer become sin. Let his days be few; and let another take his office."

We learn much about Judas in this passage. He was married and had children (vs. 9). They were cursed to remain fatherless and his wife a widow; they had to beg for bread and hide from others; others took all that his family had in their possession; no one helped them; their family tree vanished; and their sins will never be forgotten by God. This certainly is the vilest curse any human had ever received. It is no wonder that he could not contemplate life and hanged himself. He will certainly keep company with Satan himself all of eternity.

Demons. There are many references to demon activity in the Gospels. We immediately notice that every time the word "devils" appear in the plural form (if referring to demons) it is never Satan, because there is only one

Satan. We also notice that beginning with Acts, all entries of "devil" are always referring to Satan, not demons. Demons are spirit beings or angels that rebelled with Satan (Matt. 25:41). There are active demons (Eph. 6:11–12), and there are confined demons (Luke 8:31). There are demons that are temporarily confined, and there are demons that are permanently confined.

Chafer has this to say about demons in volume 2 of *Systematic Theology*. First: That this host is made up of bodiless spirits only (Matt. 12:43–45; Mark 12). Second: They are, however, not only seeking to enter the bodies of either mortals or beasts (for their power seems to be in some measure dependent upon such embodiment), but they are constantly seen to be embodied thus, according to the New Testament (Matt. 8:16, 9:32–33; Acts 8:6–7, 16:16; Mark 5:1–13). Third: They are wicked, unclean, and vicious. Many passages might be quoted in proof of this statement (Matt. 8:28, 10:1, 12:43–45).

> Demon influence, like the activity of Satan, is prompted by two motives: both to hinder the purpose of God for humanity, and to extend the authority of Satan. . . . Their influence is exercised both to mislead the unsaved and to wage an unceasing warfare against the believer (Eph. 6:12).
>
> —*Systematic Theology, Vol. 2,* p. 121

Demons also have the power to cause blindness (Matt. 12:22), dumbness (Matt. 9:32), and personal injury (Mark 9:18). Edward Gibbon demonstrates the early church belief in demons as he quotes Justin Martyr:

> Those rebellious spirits who had been degraded from the ranks of angels and cast down into the infernal pit were still permitted to roam upon the earth to torment the bodies of and to seduce the minds of sinful men. The demons soon discovered and abused the natural propensity of the human heart towards devotion, and, artfully withdrawing the adoration of mankind from their Creator, they usurped the place and honors of the Supreme Deity. By the success of their malicious contrivances they at once gratified their own vanity and revenge, and obtained the only comfort of which they were yet susceptible—the hope of involving the human species in the participation of their guilt and misery. It was confessed, or at least it was imagined, that they had distributed among themselves the most important characters of polytheism—one demon assuming the name and attributes of Jupiter, another of Aesculapius; a third, of Venus; and a fourth, perhaps, of Apollo.
>
> —*The History of the Decline and Fall of the Roman Empire, Vol.* 2, p. 89

He adds of Tertullian: "It was the universal sentiment both of the Church and of heretics that the demons were the authors, the patrons, and the objects of idolatry."

There is demon possession and there is demon influence. Demon possession is not the same as demon influence. Most scriptural references involve demon possession. Demon possession takes place when a demon or demons actually take up residence in a human body and control that individual. Demon influence involves the act of a demon or demons exerting influence on a person from the outside. Demonic activity involves either demon possession and/or demon influence.

Demons are not merely concepts that exist in our minds, they are real persons. They have intelligence because they knew who the Lord was while He was here on earth (Mark 1:24) and they knew the plan of salvation (Jam. 2:19). When confronted with judgment, they exhibited emotion (Luke 8:28; Jam. 2:19). They have wills, as expressed in Luke 8:32. They also have a personality as seen by their being addressed by personal pronouns (Luke 8:27–30).

There are many today that claim to have the ability to exorcise demons from humans. It must be noted that exorcism and casting out of demons is not the same thing. Of this Killen states:

> The exercise of exorcism consisted in the use of magical words and ceremonies for the purpose of expelling demons or evil spirits. It should be very clearly distinguished from the ministry of Christ in casting out evil spirits since He did so by His own power and authority. When His disciples cast them out in His name, they were depending upon this same power and authority (cf. Acts 3:6).
>
> —*Wycliffe Bible Encyclopedia, Vol. 1,* p. 577

It seems reasonable today, therefore, that the only way to expel demons is to cast them out, not exorcise them. It is also reasonable that the way to cast out demons is to win the possessed person to Jesus Christ, not to repeat some magical incantation over them. This would make every Christian a potential instrument in the casting out of demons. Scripture seems to teach that both the Holy Spirit and an evil spirit will not occupy the same person at the same time.

Jesus addresses this question in Matthew 12:43–45. In this narrative Jesus is describing a man that has attempted to reform himself without God's help. He tried to turn over a new leaf—much like a New Year's resolution. He was possessed by a demon. Perhaps feeling uncomfortable with the new conditions, the demon left and wandered about looking for another body to possess. He didn't find a more suitable body and decided to return to the same man that by now had cleaned up his life. He took with him seven of his demon friends even more evil than himself.

This passage not only teaches us that there are some demons more evil than others, but the unregenerated man is always susceptible to possession. Man by himself cannot pull himself up by his bootstraps and improve his moral position before God. Demons enjoy the depths of degradation but must have a human body to participate. Here, the demons participate through embodiment of a human. In contrast, the angels of Genesis 6 directly participated with humans in sin and were confined for their participation. Possibly the other demons learned from the experience and decided not to follow in their footsteps.

This passage also teaches that if the demons had returned and found the body indwelled by the Holy Spirit that they could not have re-entered. Why? We find the answer in 1 John 3:8: "For this purpose the Son of God was manifested, that he might destroy the works of the devil." Christ is the Light of the world and sheds this light abroad wherever He abides. Satan is the prince of darkness and can be overcome only by light. The light of Christ exposes darkness and it cannot exist where this light shines. Therefore, Satan or his demons cannot exist in a person where Christ dwells.

The formula for casting out demons is given in Matthew 12:25–31. In this passage, Jesus explains that the only way to occupy a house that contains a strong man is to bind him and then to cast him out. Then and only then can you occupy that house. As long as the strong man is free to re-enter, he is a constant threat. In this case the text concerns casting Satan out of a human-house. Satan is powerful and one cannot of himself accomplish this task. However, the Holy Spirit is capable of binding Satan and casting him out of the human-house. When a person appeals to God to deliver him from Satan and save his soul, the Holy Spirit binds Satan and moves into the person to dwell. The Holy Spirit then becomes the strong man and Satan cannot re-enter.

Demons increase Satan's sphere of influence by doing his bidding as presented in Ephesians 6:11–12:

> Put on the whole armour of God, that ye may be able to stand against the wiles of the devil. For we wrestle not against flesh and blood, but against principalities, against powers, against the rulers of the darkness of this world, against spiritual wickedness in high places.

Not only are demons used by Satan, they are also used

at times to accomplish God's purposes, as with Paul in 2 Corinthians 12:7. "And lest I should be exalted above measure through the abundance of the revelations, there was given to me a thorn in the flesh, the messenger of Satan to buffet me, lest I should be exalted above measure." The term "messenger" in this passage is the Greek word *anggelos,* which is the generic term for messenger. This messenger is certain to be a fallen angel (demon) under the direction of Satan allowed by God to control Paul's pride.

Demons are able to influence the minds of teachers with false doctrine as reported in 1 Timothy 4:1. "Now the Spirit speaketh expressly, that in the latter times some shall depart from the faith, giving heed to seducing spirits, and doctrines of devils."

The effects of demon possession are as varied as the many that are possessed. Unger states:

> In ordinary temptation and the usual assaults of Satan, the human will yields consciously, and, by yielding, gradually assumes, without forfeiture of its evident freedom of action, the characteristics of the Satanic nature. It is allured, solicited, and persuaded, despite the strivings of divine grace, but *not overborne.* But in demon possession, at least of the spontaneous or involuntary type, the victim seems to undergo a complete or incomplete deprivation of reason or the power of choice, with his personality so eclipsed or overwhelmed as to produce the consciousness of a twofold will in him.
>
> —*Biblical Demonology,* p. 93

The question most asked by Christians concerning demon possession is: "Can a Christian be demon possessed?" Although we see many cases of demon possession in the Gospels, we believe it to be impossible for Satan or demons to possess a child of God.

> The very nature of the believer's salvation, as embracing the regenerating, sealing, indwelling, and filling ministry of the Holy Spirit, placing him "in Christ," eternally and unforfeitably, is sufficient explanation why he is not liable to demon inhabitation.
>
> —*Biblical Demonology,* p. 100

The unbeliever, however, does not have this protection and is certainly a target for Satan.

Maniac of Gadara. In the Gospels, demon possession is often the reason for blindness, dumbness, palsy, sickness, and diseases, plus insanity, as seen in the maniac of Gadara. In Luke 8:26, Matthew 8:28–34, and Mark 5:1–17, we read of the ministry of Jesus expelling demons. The Matthew account tells of two men, but the others tell only of the one.

> And they came over unto the other side of the sea, into the country of the Gadarenes. And when he was come out of the ship, immediately there met him out of the tombs a man with an unclean spirit, Who had his dwelling among the tombs; and no man could bind him, no, not with chains: Because that he had been often bound with fetters and chains, and the chains had been plucked asunder by him, and the fetters bro-

> ken in pieces: neither could any man tame him. And always, night and day, he was in the mountains, and in the tombs, crying, and cutting himself with stones.
>
> —Mark 5:1–5

Here is a man that is possessed by many demons (vs. 9). He had superhuman strength that could break chains and no man could calm him down. He was tormented by this condition and even tortured himself with sharp stones. The demons were so many that they called themselves "Legion" (three thousand to six thousand—the largest number of a Roman army, according to the *Ryrie Study Bible*). Notice that the demons are speaking in an audible voice rather than the man (vs. 7). They also recognized Jesus and knew His power over them (vs. 7).

In Luke 8:31–32, the demons begged Jesus not to send them into the deep, or the abyss (Rev. 20:1–3) where all evil spirits will ultimately end up. They instead asked Jesus to send them into a herd of swine feeding nearby. The swine immediately ran down the hill into the lake and drowned. When demons are cast out, are they sent to the abyss? Unger thinks so when he says: "It seems reasonable to deduce from this plea, that it was at least habitual for Jesus in His expulsions to reduce the population of the free demons by dismissing them to the abyss" (*Biblical Demonology,* p. 55).

It seems that Jesus not only reduced the number of free demons, He also reduced the number of unclean animals from the countryside. What could be worse than a herd of demon-possessed swine in Israel? In volume 3 of *A Commentary,* we read that Brown believes the demons begged to be cast into the swine in hopes of leaving them and once again seeking a human to possess and continue their filthy habits.

Guardian Angels. The idea of guardian angels comes from Matthew 18:10. "Take heed that ye despise not one of these little ones; for I say unto you, That in heaven their angels do always behold the face of my Father which is in heaven." Psalm 91:11 speaks of God's protection when he says: "For he shall give his angels charge over thee, to keep thee in all thy ways." Many believe that these verses are saying that every child has been assigned a holy angel to constantly be his or her companion and keep them from harm. However, is this what the Bible means?

Certainly, we would not disagree that all children are assigned holy angels and are waiting for the Father to give them permission or instruction to act in their behalf, but can they intervene at will? We must also assume that these holy angels are recalled as these children become adults and are not saved. Once they become responsible for their sins and reject Christ, they must live without the possibility of help.

Brown states that the Lord probably meant that since these angels had charge over these little ones, they had free access into the presence of God and had a familiarity with the Father in representing them. In the *Wycliffe Bible Encyclopedia,* Killen writes that a guardian angel is one who is assigned to watch over each believer and to represent him in heaven. The writer of Hebrews asks: "Are they not all ministering spirits, sent forth to minister for them who shall be heirs of salvation?" (Heb. 1:14).

These angels minister in behalf of, not to, the heirs of salvation.

Although there is some information about guardian angels in the Bible, there are also mistaken ideas about guardian angels. Many people try to build a case for guardian angels from Matthew 4:6, and again from 18:10. However, does every individual have a guardian angel, or just specific ones who are assigned by God? Certainly there would appear to be enough angels to go around, but does God just give them direction as He sees fit?

In Matthew 4:6 we read: "And [Satan] saith unto him, If thou be the Son of God, cast thyself down: for it is written, He shall give his angels charge concerning thee." Many use this verse to claim that all Christians have guardian angels.

However, we see that the angels did not interfere with the testing of Jesus to shield Him from Satan. In Matthew 4:11 we read, "Then the devil leaveth him, and, behold, angels came and ministered unto him." These ministering spirits did not intervene in Jesus' behalf and only came to comfort Him after His ordeal. Holy angels cannot and dare not interfere with the will of God. Only in such cases as Peter's deliverance from prison (Acts 13) are angels involved in a preventative role. Does this mean that angels never intervene or cannot intervene in human affairs? Absolutely not! It does show that angels do not always intervene in human events. Here it was God's purpose that caused this direct intervention.

Another example is found in the story of the rich man and Lazarus in Luke 16:22–23:

> And it came to pass, that the beggar died, and was carried by the angels into Abraham's bosom: the rich man also died, and was buried: And in hell he lift up his eyes, being in torments, and seeth Abraham afar off, and Lazarus in his bosom.

The proof that Lazarus was acceptable under the Law lies in the fact that he was taken to Abraham's bosom, or paradise. We see that in this instance that while Lazarus was alive the angels did nothing to make his life more bearable; they did not intervene. However, after his trial was complete the angels came and ministered to him much in the same way the angels ministered to Jesus after His trial. The text says nothing about the rich man being escorted by the angels, holy or evil. We may glean from this narrative that God doesn't always intercede in behalf of the individual's testing and only ministers to him after his course is complete. The lost individual, in this case the rich man, at death is left alone to find his way to his reward. Although the text does not say, he may have been escorted by demons.

Again, looking to Matthew 18:10: we read "Take heed that ye despise not one of these little ones; for I say unto you, That in heaven their angels do always behold the face of my Father which is in heaven." Some say that this means that every child is appointed an angel to look after them, but it would seem that these angels beholding the face of God, not the children, are just awaiting directions; awaiting orders on what to do. There are so many things that are happening to children in the world today, and if they all have guardian angels, then their guardian angels must be asleep, or just not paying attention. It is believed that, at times, there is angelic intervention in the lives of children, as well as in the lives of adult Christians. However, others believe that this does not mean that every child has a guardian angel until he reaches the age of accountability, and then is abandoned.

For example, we remember what happened to the children in the Holocaust. Over one and one-half million Jewish children were murdered during World War II. If these children had angels guarding over them, then what were they doing when these children were mutilated and dying such horrible deaths in the gas chambers? What about the children in the United States who are being molested, raped, and abused, and children in Africa who are dying of starvation?

The problem may lie in the fact that Matthew 18 is addressing a situation involving the kingdom of heaven or the Millennium. At that time Christ will rule from His throne in a physical kingdom. In this passage, Christ is comparing the child of God to a child, and this child is called "one of these little ones." These are of the same ones who are called "a little child" that will exist during the kingdom of heaven. Verse 10 is a warning to those who might offend "one of these little ones" and we are told that these angels are not facing or observing the children, but are facing the Father. This may give us a different perspective regarding the disposition of these angels. They may well be angels of retribution rather than angels of intervention or guardian angels. Why are they waiting? For directions from the Father concerning those that would offend His children. We must conclude that the term "guardian angel" is not a teaching of the New Testament and does not appear in any text.

We know that there is angelic intervention in our lives by assignment. If a person is in the will of God, and it is to God's glory that this person continue in service, then certainly there is no disputing angelic intervention. So, the intervening angels (and we know they do exist in particular cases) are not the norm, but instead the exception. This intervention, or protection, is by special assignment or special mission.

The dispensation of the Mosiac Law closes with the ascension of the Lord in the first chapter of Acts. In Acts 1:10–11 we read of this event.

> And while they looked stedfastly toward heaven as he went up, behold, two men stood by them in white apparel; Which also said, Ye men of Galilee, why stand ye gazing up into heaven? this same Jesus, which is taken up from you into heaven, shall so come in like manner as ye have seen him go into heaven.

These two men dressed in white were assuredly the same ones spoken of in the four Gospels. In Matthew 28:2–3, it is said to be an angel dressed in raiment as white as snow. In Mark 16:5, the angel is described as a young man clothed in a long, white garment. In Luke 24:4, there are two men dressed in shining garments. In John 20:12, they are described as two angels in white. The term "angel" and "men" are interchanged in the Gospels and are certain to be the two men or angels at the ascension on Mount Olivet. Those that only mention one angel are surely speaking of the angel that did the communicating.

The Ministry of Angels Under the Dispensation of Grace

The dispensation grace begins in Acts 2 with the birth of the Church as we know it today. It was the fulfillment of the Jewish Feast of Passover.

> The fourth of the annual feasts of the Jews (after Passover, Unleavened Bread, and Firstfruits), it came 50 days after Firstfruits (a type of the resurrection of Christ, 1 Cor. 15:23). Pentecost was the Greek name for the Jewish Feast of Weeks, so called because it fell seven (a week of) weeks after Firstfruits. It celebrated the wheat harvest (Ex. 23:16). This Day of Pentecost in Acts 2 marked the beginning of the church (Matt. 16:18).
>
> —*Ryrie Study Bible,* p. 1635

Dr. Noah Hutchings has this to say about the dispensation of grace.

> Of the dispensation of grace, which is the hidden dispensation of mystery, we read in Acts 15:14–16, ". . . God at the first did visit the Gentiles, to take out of them a people for his name. And to this agree the words of the prophets; as it is written, After this I will return, and will build again the tabernacle of David, which is fallen down; and I will build again the ruins thereof, and I will set it up." According to this proph-

> ecy, the dispensation of grace came with the passing of Israel as a nation and the dispersion of the Jews. It will end with the refounding of Israel as a nation and their regathering (Rom. 11). The fullness, or completion of the Gentile church age occurs at the translation of the church body to Heaven (1 Thess. 4:13–18). This translation is also called the Rapture. In a sense, the sixth dispensation, the dispensation of grace, ends with another failure of man: apostasy within Christendom; population explosion with added billions going to Hell; as in Noah's day, crime and perversion filling the earth; and man himself threatening to destroy the world (1 Tim. 4:1–2; 2 Tim. 3:1–9; 2 Pet. 2–3; Matt. 24:37; Rev. 11:18).
>
> —*Why So Many Churches?*, p. 23

There are many who believe that the Church began at another time prior to Acts 2. The following is seminary notes taken from Dr. Charles Hauser. There are four reasons that the Church began in Acts 2. First, in Colossians 1:24, we see the Church is the body of Christ. Second, in 1 Corinthians 12:13, we find that we get into the body of Christ through the baptism of the Holy Spirit. Third, in Acts 1:5, we see the promised baptism of the Holy Spirit still yet future; no baptism, no body. Fourth, in Acts 11:15–16, we read that the baptism of the Holy Spirit began at Pentecost. What happened to Cornelius in Acts 10, happened to us in Acts 2. Based upon these four steps, the Church as we know it today began at Pentecost. It is here that we begin our study of angels in the age of grace.

The Kingdom of Heaven. One of the problems in dealing with the dispensation of grace is the misunderstanding of the difference between the kingdom of heaven and the kingdom of God. Since the purpose of this study is not to dwell on the difference, we will simply give the definitions of the two kingdoms. The kingdom of heaven is the message that Jesus preached to the Jews prior to His crucifixion. This kingdom is a physical kingdom with Christ as its physical King. This is the message that John the Baptist came preaching in Matthew 3:2: "Repent ye: for the kingdom of heaven is at hand."

The Jewish people in Christ's day were looking for a messiah to rule over them in a kingdom. John told them that they would have to "repent" in order for this kingdom to begin. That became a stumbling block to them and they rejected the King, therefore rejecting the kingdom. Jesus began to preach about this kingdom in Matthew 4:17. "Repent: for the kingdom of heaven is at hand." He continued to preach about this kingdom in Matthew 5, with the Sermon on the Mount.

Jesus made a valid offer of the kingdom to the Jews. Had they accepted Him as their King, the kingdom would have been ushered in after a time of Tribulation to purge Israel and judge the nations, but they ultimately rejected Jesus as their Messiah and killed Him. He announced to Israel that He had tried to gather Israel as a hen gathered her chicks, but they would not listen (Matt. 23:37). Then, in Matthew 23:39, He announced His decision to reject them until they repented. "For I say unto you, Ye shall not see me henceforth, till ye shall say, Blessed is he that cometh in the name of the Lord." This repentance will take place at the close of the Tribulation period.

He immediately departed from the Temple and began His discourse on the Tribulation and Millennium passages in Matthew 24 and 25. The kingdom of heaven and the Millennium (one thousand years) are the same, and will take place after the age of grace. It represents a system of faith and works, is temporal in its duration, and is confined to the earth in its scope.

Peter continued to preach the gospel of the kingdom of heaven to the Jews, while Paul preached the gospel of the death, burial, and resurrection of Christ. Hutchings again has his finger on the pulse of the difference between what Paul and Peter were preaching when he says:

> Peter preached, as recorded in Acts 3:19–20: "Repent ye therefore, and be converted, that your sins may be blotted out, when the times of refreshing [the Kingdom of Heaven] shall come from the presence of the Lord; And he shall send Jesus Christ, which before was preached unto you." Peter preached that if Israel would repent and receive Christ as Lord, God would send Him back to bring in the Kingdom. Peter's message envisioned a return of Christ upon repentance in Israel to personally blot out their sins.
>
> —*Why So Many Churches,* p. 39

Peter was clearly preaching the kingdom of heaven after the beginning of the Church.

The kingdom of heaven refers to an earthly reign by heaven, not in heaven. This kingdom is spoken of by Daniel (Dan. 2:44) in the Old Testament, and by Christ in the New Testament. Christ is to be the rightful heir to the throne of this kingdom. It is a sphere of profession, and contains both the saved and the unsaved as seen in the parables of the wheat and tares in Matthew 13:24, and the good and bad fish of Matthew 13:47.

It is interesting to note that men are never told to seek this kingdom, but are told to seek the kingdom of God (Matt. 6:33; Luke 12:31). The kingdom of God is not a dispensation, but the kingdom of heaven is a dispensation. Finally, the saved element of the kingdom of heaven is placed within the kingdom of God. It will become swallowed up by the kingdom of God (1 Cor. 15:24–28). Both the kingdom of heaven and the kingdom of God are contained in the universal sphere of God, which contains all of creation. "The LORD hath prepared his throne in the heavens; and his kingdom ruleth over all" (Ps. 103:19).

The Kingdom of God. The kingdom of God is universal in scope and involves a spiritual reign. The godly are the subjects and God is the King. It is a sphere of possession, not profession, and contains only saved elements (John 3:5). The kingdom of God is near (Luke 10:9); contains mysteries (Mark 4:11); contains only the saved (Matt. 13:24–30); contains rapid growth (Mark 4:30–32); is likened unto children (Mark 10:14); will come with power (Mark 9:1); is difficult to enter (Mark 10:23, 25); is where Christ will drink of the fruit of the vine with the saints (Mark 14:25); contains certain blessings to the righteous (Luke 6:20); contains satanic influences (Mark 4:30); is hidden as leaven in meal (Luke 13:20–21); is characterized by righteousness and peace (Rom. 14:17); is delivered to the Father (1 Cor. 15:24); and is to be inherited by incorruptible beings (1 Cor. 15:50). Again, men are told to seek the kingdom of God, but not the kingdom of heaven.

The Ministry of Angels During the Church. In the Church age, the activity of angels seems to become less active than during the time of the Law. During this time the term "angel" appears thirty-one times; "angels," thirty-one times; "unclean spirits," two times; "demon," sixteen times; "demons," six times; "Satan," sixteen times; and "Michael the archangel," twice. In the books written concerning the Church, Acts and Hebrews represent thirty-four of the sixty-two times that the holy angels are mentioned. Angels are not mentioned in Ephesians, Philippians, 1 Thessalonians, 2 Timothy, Titus, Philemon, James, and 1, 2, and 3 John. Why is the ministry of angels suddenly less active than under the Law?

In the Old Testament, and particularly under the Law, God communicated to man through His messengers, the angels. In the Church age the messenger service of the angels is not needed for God to communicate with the saints. We now receive our communication from God directly through the indwelling ministry of the Holy Spirit.

In John 14:26 Jesus promised the coming of the Holy Spirit. "But the Comforter, which is the Holy Ghost, whom the Father will send in my name, he shall teach you all things, and bring all things to your remembrance, whatsoever I have said unto you." As the disciples did not need angels while in the presence of Jesus, we as Christians do not need the angels as messengers because we have the indwelling ministry of the Holy Spirit.

"Know ye not that ye are the temple of God, and that the Spirit of God dwelleth in you?" (1 Cor. 3:16). The Holy Spirit also regenerates us (Titus 3:5); baptizes us (1 Cor. 12:13); and seals us (Eph. 1:13). All four of these events happened at the moment of salvation. To prove that these things actually happened between ourselves and the Lord, His spirit bears witness with our spirit (Rom. 8:16).

The enabling Holy Spirit also "fills us" or "empowers us" to perform specific tasks that He has called us to do (Eph. 5:18). Filling and indwelling are two entirely different actions by God. In the Old Testament, men were filled to perform and it was only temporary. In the age of grace men are also filled to perform and it is temporary. However, indwelling is unique to this age and it is permanent. The Spirit is the secret to victory.

With the help of the Holy Spirit, we do not need added revelation or the help of angels. "But ye have an unction [anointing] from the Holy One, and ye know all things" (1 John 2:20). The Holy Spirit also intercedes in our behalf. "Likewise the Spirit also helpeth our infirmities: for we know not what we should pray for as we ought: but the Spirit itself maketh intercession for us with groanings which cannot be uttered" (Rom. 8:26).

Some take this verse to mean that the Holy Spirit enables them to talk directly to the Father through the means of some ecstatic language. This could not be farther from the truth. As Christ intercedes for us at the right hand of the Father, the Holy Spirit intercedes on our behalf from the inside. The agent here is the Holy Spirit, not the person. The Holy Spirit voices our needs on our behalf, based on the will of God. While I may not know what I need, the Holy Spirit does, and conveys that need to God. We are at times unable to understand or know how to pray. But in this age we do not need angels to be a messenger from God.

Unclean and Evil Spirits. The term "unclean spirits" occurs in this period in Acts 5:16 and Acts 8:7, and "evil spirits" in Acts 19:12–13 and 16. We read in Acts 5:16: "There came also a multitude out of the cities round about unto Jerusalem, bringing sick folks, and them which were vexed with unclean spirits: and they were healed every one." Unlike the supposed healing services today, every person who came, regardless of their station in life or their malady, was healed without exception. These unclean and evil spirits were demons that had taken up residence in these people. These people were not only healed physically, but were also healed spiritually.

We also notice that these were Jews and not Gentiles. Peter always preached to Israel and was evidently preaching on the resurrection, because the Sadducees were incensed and had the apostles arrested. The Sadducees neither believed in the resurrection or angels, so it seems ironic that an angel from the Lord freed them.

In Acts 13:10 we read of one that is called the "child of the devil." Paul and Barnabas were witnessing to Sergius Paulus, the deputy of Paphos, when Bar-Jesus [Elymas] tried to turn the deputy away from the faith. Paul called Elymas the "child of the devil." The word for devil is *diabolos,* the same word used for Satan. Paul did not mean that he was actually Satan's child, but the devil's advocate.

Other entries of demons in the Church age are: concerning sacrificing to demons (1 Cor. 10:20); having fellowship with demons (1 Cor. 10:20); the cup of demons and the table of demons (1 Cor. 10:21); the doctrines of demons (1 Tim. 4:1); and demons believing (Jam. 2:19).

Satan. Satan is very active in opposition to the Christians during the Church age. All entries that refer to Satan as a devil concern our resisting him. We are told to never give place to the devil (Eph. 4:27); stand against the wiles of the devil (Eph. 6:11); concerning the condemnation reproach and snare of the devil (1 Tim. 3:6–7); recovering from the snare of the devil (2 Tim. 2:26); the power of death concerning the devil (Heb. 2:14); resisting the devil (Jam. 4:7); your adversary the devil (1 Pet. 5:8); sin and the works of sin is of the devil (1 John 3:8); the children of the devil (1 John 3:10); contending with the devil (Jude 9); and concerning the devil casting some into prison (Rev. 2:10).

Ananias and Sapphira. The remaining entries concern direct actions by Satan. In Acts 5:1 we read of Ananias and his wife Sapphira, who sold a parcel of land with the goal of sharing the price with the church. The two conspired together and lied not only to Peter, but most importantly to the Holy Spirit. They were not required to sell the property or give anything to the church. However, through greed or fear of the future, they lied about the price. Peter immediately recognized the deception and confronted Ananias, saying that Satan had influenced him to lie; not lying to Peter but to God, because the Holy Ghost [Spirit] is God. Ananias upon hearing of his discovery fell dead. Later his wife Sapphira met with the same fate. Satan was the culprit, even though every man is a liar (Rom. 3:4), because Satan is a liar and the father of liars (John 8:44).

Church Discipline. We read of angelic activity concerning church discipline in 1 Corinthians 5:5. "To deliver such an one unto Satan for the destruction of the flesh, that the spirit may be saved in the day of the Lord Jesus." This individual was guilty of a sin so vile that even those that worship idols would not be guilty of committing or even considering it. He had taken his father's wife, possibly even his own mother or stepmother. This passage is a good example of how God uses Satan to chasten Christians much the same way as He worked with Israel in the Old Testament.

Matthew Henry states:

> This was not a common instance of fornication, but *such as was not so much as named among the Gentiles, that a man should have his father's wife*—either marry her while his father was alive, or keep her as his concubine, either when he was dead or while he was alive. In either of these cases, his criminal conversation with her might be called *fornication;* but had his father been dead, and he, after his decease, married to her, it had been incest still, but neither fornication nor adultery in the strictest sense. But to marry her, or keep her as a concubine, while his father was alive, though he had repudiated her, or she had deserted him, whether she were his own mother or not, was incestuous fornication.
>
> —*Commentary on the Whole Bible, Vol. 6,* p. 426

Paul not only has disgust for the fornicator, he is bewildered as to why the church has not dealt with the situation. The church was actually "puffed up" or had glorified this sin, and in doing so had condoned his action. Paul states that he has already judged that sin which was their responsibility. Paul could not understand why some action had not been taken. The old saying, "a man is known be the company he keeps," could also be stated of churches, "a church is known by the persons it keeps." Paul prescribed a course of action: "Therefore put away from among yourselves that wicked person" (vs. 13). We learn from this passage that God is responsible to judge those without the church (vs. 13), but the church is responsible to judge its own members (vs. 12). This man is believed to be a Christian, or else Paul would not be instructing the church to judge him.

In verse 5 we read the motive for delivering one to Satan: " . . . that the spirit may be saved in the day of the Lord Jesus." Delivering a saint to Satan is done for one of two reasons. First, when God delivered Job to Satan it was because he had already been judged faithful and his body was to be preserved. He was being tested, not to prove himself, but as a testimony to Satan, the rest of the community, and we ourselves. In the end Job was paid the highest tribute for his faithfulness. Second, as we see here, this man was judged unfaithful and is turned over to Satan for the destruction of the body. He was not to be allowed to continue in this gross sin and remain a bad testimony to the Lord's work.

Though it is not written, it is implied that there is an umbrella of protection contained within the body of the local church. When we voluntarily or involuntarily are placed outside this umbrella of protection, we are placed directly in the presence of Satan (Eph. 6:16). To be delivered unto Satan is to be placed outside this umbrella. When we voluntarily forsake the assembling of ourselves together, we are placing ourselves outside this umbrella of protection. Paul sets the precedent for this action in Romans 14:12–13.

> So then every one of us shall give account of himself to God. Let us not therefore judge one another any more: but judge this rather, that no man put a stumblingblock or an occasion to fall in his brother's way.

Paul here is stating that God will judge our motives and sins of omission because we are unable to look into the heart and discern the intent. However, he is saying that we are to judge in matters that pertain to actions or sins of commission. When anyone becomes a stumblingblock to others individually or to the church as a whole, then we are to take action to protect the testimony and integrity of the Lord's work. This action is in the form of placing one into the domain of Satan and allowing him to do what God permits. In 1 Corinthians 11 Paul is cautioning the Christians not to violate the rules and conduct concerning the Lord's Supper. This falls under self-judgment. Some who had not judged themselves are spoken of in verse 30: "For this cause many are weak and sickly among you, and many sleep." It is not known if this is a result of being turned over to Satan, but it follows the same criteria found in other passages.

The penalty that may be meted out using Satan is mentioned in 1 John 5:16–17:

> If any man see his brother sin a sin which is not unto death, he shall ask, and he shall give him life for them that sin not unto death. There is a sin unto death: I do not say that he shall pray for it. All unrighteousness is sin: and there is a sin not unto death.

The penalty for being turned over to Satan varies from chastisement to death.

Under the dispensation of human government, capital punishment was instituted to enforce the power to govern (Gen. 9:6). The death penalty was to be carried out by the civil government for the good of all. The "body of Christ" also seems to have this power by exposing a person to Satan for some sin of commission. In 1 John 5:16–17 the early Church could discern the sins unto death and the sins not unto death. Today's Christians have become so much a part of the world that these sins are not discernible for the most part. These sins do vary in degree of punishment.

One very unlikely person to be turned over to Satan is Paul. He was a powerful Christian responsible for most of the epistles of the New Testament. Paul was evidently a proud man because of his accomplishments, for we read in 2 Corinthians 12:7: "And lest I should be exalted above measure through the abundance of the revelations, there was given to me a thorn in the flesh, the messenger of Satan to buffet me, lest I should be exalted above measure." This evidently was the sin of pride. God allowed

Satan to weaken the flesh in order to keep this pride in check. Paul recognized the origin of this punishment and asked God three times to remove it, but God would not. It was for Paul's own good and he recognized the purpose. Paul's sin was not unto death.

We read of another case concerning Satan's use in church discipline in 1 Timothy 1:19–20:

> Holding faith, and a good conscience; which some having put away concerning faith have made shipwreck: Of whom is Hymenaeus and Alexander; whom I have delivered unto Satan, that they may learn not to blaspheme.

Paul here is not speaking to a church, but to Timothy, and instructing him how to handle specific cases of church discipline. Here also Paul states the he himself as an apostle has the power to deliver one to Satan. The blasphemy of these men is discussed in 2 Timothy 2:16–18:

> But shun profane and vain babblings: for they will increase unto more ungodliness. And their word will eat as doth a canker: of whom is Hymenaeus and Philetus; Who concerning the truth have erred, saying that the resurrection is past already; and overthrow the faith of some.

If you allow a small error to creep in, then it will grow into something that will discourage and weaken the faith of some Christians.

In 2 Timothy 2:16–18 the name of Philetus is added to Hymenaeus and Alexander, and their sins were that of false teaching. They were teaching that the Rapture was already past, causing some to give up hope. What their punishment was is not disclosed. However, we assume it was not unto death because in 1 Timothy 1:20 the punishment was to teach them "not to blaspheme," not to take their life.

In 1 Corinthians 5:5 we see the severest form of punishment, possibly unto death. Satan would be allowed to destroy the flesh of the one guilty of the sin of fornication. How Satan is to administer this penalty is not known. Henry states:

> This was to be done *in the name of Christ,* with the power of Christ, and in a full assembly, where the apostle would be also present in spirit, or by his spiritual gift of discerning at a distance. Some think that this is to be understood of a mere ordinary excommunication, and that delivering him to Satan for the destruction of the flesh is only meant of disowning him, and casting him out of the church, that by this means he might be brought to repentance, and his flesh might be mortified. . . . Note, Church-censures are Christ's ordinances, and should be dispensed in his name. It was to be done also *when they were gathered together,* in full assembly. The more public the more solemn, and the more solemn the more likely to have a good effect on the offender.
>
> —*Commentary on the Whole Bible, Vol. 6,* p. 426

Ryrie says of 1 Corinthians 5:5:

> This evidently means that the church was to discipline this sinning brother by committing him to Satan's domain, the world (1 John 5:19), and to Satan's chastisement, the destruction or ruin of the body (*flesh* means "body" here) through sickness or even death. *Destruction* does not mean annihilation by ruin.
>
> —*Ryrie Study Bible,* p. 1731

Whether or not this man lost his life is unknown, but Paul did list "fornication" as one of the sins in the list of "things worthy of death" in Romans 1:29, 32. It is not our place to determine the severity of the penalty; it is our responsibility to perform church discipline. Christ gave us our formula for church discipline in Matthew 18:15–17. First, it is the responsibility of the offended to go to the offender and ask for an apology. Second, if that fails, then we are to take two or three witnesses to hear the offender. Third, if that fails, we are to take our case before the church to hear the offense. If that fails, then we are to treat the offender as a heathen, and place him outside the church. This could be construed as the equivalent of "stoning" under the Law.

In 1 John 5:16–17 we receive our instructions concerning the "sin unto death" and the "sin not unto death." We are told to pray for the life of the one that commits the "sin not unto death." We are not to pray for the death of the one that commits the "sin unto death."

In conclusion, this section on church discipline is very important because it reveals to us how angelic activity is involved. Satan is the instrument that God uses to chastise the Christian that involves himself in sin as a way of life. Even though the biblical activity of holy angels during the Church age is quiet, we can see the activity of Satan and his angels, and they must be *very* active in today's liberal churches.

Angel of Light. We also see Satan described as an "angel of light," and his workers as "ministers of righteousness" in 2 Corinthians 11:13–15.

> For such are false apostles, deceitful workers, transforming themselves into the apostles of Christ. And no marvel; for Satan himself is transformed into an angel of light. Therefore it is no great thing if his ministers also be transformed as the ministers of righteousness; whose end shall be according to their works.

In this text, Paul is defending his conduct. Paul states that he has been completely honest and open as he has served Christ. He had never placed his service to their charge for he had made tents so as not to be a burden. He speaks to them sarcastically in the questions he asks them. He stated that he even took money from other poorer churches so they would not be able to say that he preached for money. However, he states that others that preach other gospels have been motivated by money. It is no surprise to him that these charlatans appear to be godly, because the one they serve disguises himself as an angel of light.

In today's religious society there are many that present themselves as God's servants. One of these groups represents the New Age society. Fred C. Dickason has this to say about the New Agers:

> New Age proponents often consider angels as part of the energy of the universe, whom may be used to tap into our "innate powers." Clearly, however, good angels are completely obedient to God and never deceive humans, as do the spirits contacted through mediums (channelers). The "spirit guides" of those involved in the New Age or the occult are really deceptive demons posing as "angels of light."
>
> —*Names of Angels,* p. 38

These New Age angels of light do pose a threat, but mainly to the unsaved and untaught. Paul states that if any come and preach another gospel other than that which they had already received, they are angels of light, or false teachers. He is even more outspoken about the issue of false teachers in Galatians 1:8: "But though we, or an angel from heaven, preach any other gospel unto you than that which we have preached unto you, let him be accursed." The problem of false teachers in his day has not gone away today, because what worked for Satan then stills works for Satan today.

Paul's words have proven to be prophetic. Surely, God revealed to him the Church of Jesus Christ of Latter Day Saints. He could not have described them more accurately if he were alive today. They do present "another gospel" alongside of the King James Bible. This "other gospel" was given to them by the angel Moroni. It is interesting to note that this book was translated into the King James middle English. The conclusion is that they fit Paul's description of a cult, presented by Satan as an angel of light. Since they preach another gospel given by an angel, our instruction is to "let them be accursed."

The word "accursed" is translated from the Greek word *anathema,* or devoted to destruction. Some would have us to believe that this means to excommunicate a person from the Church because of his heresy. However, the fact that an angel is also included in the list of violators disqualifies this idea as mere supposition. Certainly Paul is describing the Judaizers that constantly plagued the new believers after Paul had moved on to his next missionary assignment. The method of the Judaizers is still in use today by many cults and those who name the name of Jesus to pervert His gospel. Instruction in this matter is clear. If someone brings us to any other gospel than was first preached by Paul, then we are to separate ourselves from them (human or angel) and allow them to be cursed by God. The apostle John calls these false teachers who pervert the gospel of Christ, antichrist. He instructs us not to even bid them Godspeed (goodbye) (2 John 10). He adds that if anyone bids them Godspeed, he is a partaker of his evil deeds.

The main threat to Christians is angels of light that come from those who pose as mainline denominational ministers. They each have a "special gift" that separates them from the rest of the pack, marked by special knowledge that no one else has received. They become larger than the God they are supposed to be serving. In essence these are also preaching another gospel. Theirs is not the gospel of faith in Jesus Christ as presented by the New Testament writers, but rather a gospel of works that is always sold to the highest bidders.

If money were taken out of the equation, there would

be very few new gospels, only those invented by Satan and not man. Paul tells Timothy in 1 Timothy 6:10: "For the love of money is the root of all evil: which while some coveted after, they have erred from the faith, and pierced themselves through with many sorrows." The modern-day angels of light are never interested in new converts, but proselytes from others. "Therefore it is no great thing if his ministers also be transformed as the ministers of righteousness; whose end shall be according to their works" (2 Cor. 11:15). "If their master himself, the 'prince of darkness,' the most alien to light, does so, it is less marvellous in his servants" (Fausset, *A Commentary, Vol. 3*, p. 365).

> Under the guise of the Edenic serpent, he first fashioned himself "as an angel of light" (Gen. 3:1; 2 Cor. 11:14). It would not at all be surprising, therefore, if his satellite demons should so fashion themselves, and assume the semblance of human form, should occasion so require.
>
> —*Biblical Demonology,* p. 64

What a frightful thought! Could those who present themselves as ministers, which are truly angels of light, be demons?

These angels of light would be as industrious in promoting error as the apostles were promoting the truth. These are the counterfeit prophets of the Old Testament who learned the language of the Lord, and as angels of light passed themselves off as the genuine article. "As he can turn himself into any shape, and put on almost any form, and look sometimes *like an angel of light,* in order to promote his kingdom of darkness, so he will teach his ministers and instruments to do the same" (Henry, *A Commentary on the Whole Bible, Vol. 6,* p. 514).

The Rapture of the Church. The Rapture of the Church is addressed in 1 Thessalonians 4:13–18 and 1 Corinthians 15:51–53. Some say that the word "rapture" is not in the English Bible, and they are correct, at least in part. In 1 Thessalonians 4:17 we find the term "caught up." The word for "caught up" in the Koine Greek is *harpadzo.* Translated into Latin, *harpadzo* becomes *rapturo.* When the Latin word *rapturo* is transliterated (not translated) into English it becomes "rapture." So we see that the word "rapture" actually does occur. It is much like the word "baptism." The word in the Koine Greek is *baptidzo,* "to dip or immerse." The word *baptidzo* is transliterated into the English words "to baptize."

In 1 Thessalonians 4:16 we read: "For the Lord himself shall descend from heaven with a shout, with the voice of the archangel, and with the trump of God and the dead in Christ shall rise first." It has been suggested that the voice of the archangel was necessary to call to attention all of the angelic hosts to clear the way for the ones being resurrected. These angels will be called to attention by the archangel so as not to interfere.

The Lord descending with a shout is certainly a selective shout. A general shout would empty the graves of every soul, saved or unsaved. This is why Jesus stood at the grave and shouted, "Lazarus come forth" (John 11:43). A general shout would have emptied all the graves on earth simply because of the power in His voice. The

Greek word for "cloud" in 1 Thessalonians 4:17 is *nephele,* the same word that appears in Acts 1:9 and Revelation 11:12. In some instances it means a cloud of a definite shape. Therefore, in this text it is possibly representing a cloud of witnesses, which could represent an angelic host.

Angels to the Seven Churches

The dispensation of grace continues through the third chapter of Revelation and includes the letters to the seven churches. The book was written by the Apostle John who was also the author of the Gospel of John and the three epistles of John. The contents of this book came directly from the Lord Jesus Christ and "sent and signified it by his angel unto his servant John" (Rev. 1:1). Therefore, the entire contents of the book were delivered by a holy angel.

This book is therefore "the revelation of Jesus Christ," not the revelation of John. The word translated "revelation" in 1:1, comes from the Greek word *apokalupsis.* It means "to unveil," "reveal," "to make manifest," or "to uncover to view." It therefore must be the revealment, manifestation, or appearing of Jesus Christ. So this book is meant to reveal the mind of Jesus Christ, not veil it. The phrase in verse 1, "must shortly come to pass," does not mean that it will come to pass soon, but that when it starts it will come to pass swiftly.

This is the only book in the Bible that states that a person will be blessed just for reading it. It is the only book in the New Testament that gives His endorsement and affixes His signature, saying at it closes: "I Jesus have sent mine angel to testify unto you these things in the churches" (Rev. 22:16). It is the only book that curses the person that will "add unto" or "take away" (22:18–19). One example of this exclusion is given by Edward Gibbon in *The History of the Decline and Fall of the Roman Empire.* He states concerning the Book of Revelation as a mysterious prophecy:

> The doctrine of Christ's reign upon earth was at first treated as a profound allegory; was considered by degrees as a doubtful and useless opinion; and was at length rejected as the absurd invention of heresy and fanaticism.
>
> —*The History of the Decline and Fall of the Roman Empire, Vol. 2,* p. 102

The footnote then addresses the accusation called in question by Gibbon:

> In the Council of Laodicea (about the year 360), the Apocalypse was tacitly excluded from the sacred canon by the same churches of Asia to which it is addressed; and we may learn from the complaint of Sulpicius Severus that their sentence had been ratified by the greater number of Christians of his time.

The Council of Trent (1545–63) later reinstated the Book of Revelation to the Catholic canon.

The Signifying Angel

We are not told who this angel was, but when in 22:8–9 John bowed to him he was told: "See thou do it not: for I am thy fellowservant, and of thy brethren the prophets, and of them which keep the sayings of this book." Larkin believes that this angel must be one of the old prophets raised for this purpose. Although the generic meaning of angel is "messenger," we see no indication that this one that came from God was a prophet raised from the dead. In *The Revelation of Jesus Christ,* Walvoord suggests that the angel may be Gabriel (cf. Dan. 8:16; 9:2, 21–22; Luke 1:26–31). Whoever this angel was, it is certain that he was a holy angel because he was representing the Lord Jesus Christ.

> The word rendered *signified,* taken in connection with the fact that the things signified were matters of contemplation by means of the eyes, can denote nothing else than an actual picturing of those scenes—a making of them pass before the view the same as if they were really transpiring.
>
> —Seiss, *The Apocalypse,* p. 20

The Seven Churches

The identity of the churches is varied by different writers. Bullinger states that it is erroneous to place the Church in this book.

> If these "churches" are future assemblies of Jewish believers on the earth, after the Church has been "caught up to meet the Lord," then all is clear, consistent, and easy to be understood. The real difficulty is created by attempting to read the Church into the book where is (sic) has no place.
>
> —*Commentary on Revelation,* p. 71

Seiss believes these to be seven different independent

churches. "They were organized into distinct congregations in the several towns and cities, and these separate and independent assemblies are spoken of as so many 'Churches'" (*The Apocalypse,* p. 26). Walvoord agrees with Seiss that these are seven churches that existed in the province of Asia Minor (*The Revelation of Jesus Christ,* p. 37). We must agree with Seiss and Walvoord that these churches actually existed at the time the book was written. Larkin writes that these seven churches must be representatives of typical churches for that time, but at the same time they represent seven church periods clearly defined in church history.

Notes in the *Scofield Reference Bible* go a step farther than Larkin. He writes that the seven churches of Revelation have a fourfold application. First, the local churches actually addressed; second, admonitory, to all churches in all time as tests; third, a personal exhortation to the one "that hath an ear"; and fourth, prophetic, as disclosing the seven of the spiritual church unto the end. Scofield seems to be correct in his assertion because all four elements are contained within the text of the seven churches.

In visiting this area found in Turkey, we found that all the sites still exist, some more extensive than others, but all are being rebuilt. The most extravagant of these is the city of Ephesus. These churches are identified in chapters two and three as Ephesus, Smyrna, Pergamos, Thyatira, Sardis, Philadelphia, and Laodicea.

The Seven Spirits

In 1:4 we read: "Grace be unto you, and peace, from him

which is, and which was, and which is to come; and from the seven Spirits which are before his throne." Though this verse speaks of the three time periods that are affected, the identity of the seven spirits is not told. The number seven is very significant in the book of Revelation. Throughout the Bible this number has signified the number of completion, or perfection. Here in Revelation it is used for these seven spirits (1:4); the seven candlesticks (1:12); the seven horns and seven eyes of the Lamb (5:6); the seven angels and seven trumpets (8:2); the seven thunders (10:3); the seven heads of the dragon (12:3); the seven heads of the beast (13:1); the seven golden vials (15:7); and the seven kings (17:10).

Seiss states in *The Apocalypse* that the seven spirits are representative of the Holy Spirit in the full completeness of His office and powers. Most writers completely omit the identity of the seven spirits. If Seiss is referring to Isaiah 11:2, then we might agree with him. Here in this verse we see the sevenfold Spirit of the Lord. "And the spirit of the LORD [1] shall rest upon him, the spirit of wisdom [2] and understanding [3], the spirit of counsel [4] and might [5], the spirit of knowledge [6] and of the fear [7] of the LORD." Even though some try to give the identity of the seven spirits to that of angels, it is evident that the Holy Spirit is meant here.

The Seven Stars

"And he had in his right hand seven stars: and out of his mouth went a sharp two-edged sword: and his countenance was as the sun shineth in his strength" (Rev. 1:16). The identity of the seven stars is answered in verse 20.

"The mystery of the seven stars which thou sawest in my right hand, and the seven golden candlesticks. The seven stars are the angels of the seven churches: and the seven candlesticks which thou sawest are the seven churches." The mystery of the identity of the seven stars is answered, but what is the identity of the seven messengers? Are we looking at angelic activity or human activity?

In *The Revelation of Jesus Christ* Wolvoord writes that these seven messengers refer to the leaders of the churches to whom the primary messages were sent. It is possible that these seven pastors traveled to Patmos. The spiritual significance of these seven messengers is that they were responsible for the spiritual warfare of these churches. The *Scofield Reference Bible* states that the most natural explanation is that they are men sent to Patmos to ascertain the welfare of the Apostle John. It is agreed that these were not angels, but were men and probably the pastors of the seven churches. Each pastor was given a message to his church that applied to its spiritual condition, and the future church it represented.

Chapter Seven

The Ministry of Angels During the Tribulation Period

Chapter five opens the Tribulation, and with it a sudden surge of angelic activity. The Church has been removed at the Rapture, and with it the indwelling and restraining ministry of the Holy Spirit (2 Thess. 2). Daniel's "seventieth week" is now beginning with impending urgency. Satan knows his time is short and he will increase his demonic activity to try to overcome the saints and delay his inevitable doom. The Lord will counter with the holy angels to defeat Satan and his forces. The purpose of the Tribulation period is to purge Israel and judge the nations. It will be a period of unprecedented warfare and destruction that will try the world and man. The method of conveyance and delivery of messages, as well as the messengers, will be angels, both holy and unholy.

The Strong Angel

We begin the Tribulation period with Revelation 5:1–2.

> And I saw in the right hand of him that sat on the throne a book written within and on the backside, sealed with seven seals. And I saw a strong angel proclaiming with a loud voice, Who is worthy to open the book, and to loose the seals thereof?

The angel in verse 2 is not the one who is to open the seals; he is only the one that is asking with a voice that penetrates even the depths of hell: "Who is worthy to open the book?" "Strong" is from a Greek word *ischyros,* which means "mighty" or "powerful." It is used here and also in 10:1 and 18:21. On page 114 of *The Revelation of Jesus Christ,* Walvoord cites J. B. Smith, who says that his loud voice means urgency and great concern. Smith states that this can be only Gabriel, the one who ordered the opening and closing of the book of Daniel.

This angel was announcing himself as the champion of the King. If he himself was not worthy or strong enough to open the seals, then what created being was worthy? He dared anyone to step forward and proclaim himself worthy to claim the prize. David said of the angels in Psalm 103:20: "Bless the LORD, ye his angels, that excel in strength, that do his commandments, hearkening unto the voice of his word." In Revelation 5:11 the beasts and elders are joined by "ten thousand times ten thousand, and thousands of thousands" of angels who said with a loud voice: "Worthy is the Lamb that was slain to receive power, and riches, and wisdom, and strength, and honour, and glory, and blessing" (Rev. 5:12).

At the beginning of the sixth chapter we see the start

of the opening of the seal judgments. The first four seals are represented by what is commonly called the "four horsemen of the apocalypse." Although these are not angels, and are not representing angels, it may be important for the continuity to mention them. The first rides a white horse, is given a crown and a bow, and sets about to conquer. He is the Antichrist. The second rides a red horse, was given a "great sword," and "power" was given to him "to take peace from the earth." The third rides a black horse, is given a set of balances, and sets about to establish the economic system. The fourth rides a pale horse, was given a sword, and sets about to kill one-fourth the population of the earth.

The Four Angels

In Revelation 7:1 we read: "And after these things I saw four angels standing on the four corners of the earth, holding the four winds of the earth, that the wind should not blow on the earth, nor on the sea, nor on any tree."

These angels were standing by about to bring wrath upon the earth. Some have suggested that if the wind does not blow, then life will begin to die. These angels are joined by another angel from the east that has the seal of the living God. The four angels are to postpone what they are doing until the angels (vs. 3) had time to seal the foreheads of the 144,000 Jews with the seal of the living God. The angel cried with a loud voice to call all angelic activity to cease until his task was complete. We do not know if these four angels were holy angels or fallen angels, but the holy angel from the east had authority over them.

Angels of the Seven Trumpets

The next group of angels are introduced in 8:1–3:

> And when he had opened the seventh seal, there was silence in heaven about the space of half an hour. And I saw the seven angels which stood before God; and to them were given seven trumpets. And another angel came and stood at the altar, having a golden censer; and there was given unto him much incense, that he should offer it with the prayers of all saints upon the golden altar which was before the throne.

This chapter opens with deadly silence interceding a time that events are happening at trip-hammer speed. This must be the most important event to happen to this point. These angels are said to be standing in the presence of God, and must have much power and authority as shown by Gabriel in Luke 1:19. Another angel which came and stood at the altar and was given much incense is said by some to be the angelic representation of Christ. However, he had to be given the ability and instruments to worship, which would preclude Christ.

> Attention is also directed in verse 5 to the censer, apparently corresponding to the instrument used to offer incense in the Old Testament worship. It was made of gold (Exodus 37:25–28; Heb. 9:4), and it was used to take fire off the altar to be carried into the Holy of Holies where the incense was added. Here the angel is said to take the censer filled with fire and cast it into the earth. This incident is followed by voices,

> thunderings, lightnings, and an earthquake. The clear implication is that the censer is here used as a symbol of judgment, apparently in response to the intercession and prayers of the suffering saints in the midst of the great tribulation. The scene, therefore, is set for the judgment symbolized by the seven trumpets about to sound according to verse 6.
>
> —Walvoord, *The Revelation of Jesus Christ,* p. 153

The seventh seal (vs. 1) contains the seven trumpets (vs. 6). The first angel sounded, and hail and fire mingled with blood were cast to the earth, and one-third of the "trees was burnt up, and all green grass was burnt up." The second angel sounded, and a great mountain of fire "was cast into the sea"; one-third of the sea became blood; and one-third of the creatures died, and one-third of the ships were destroyed. The third angel sounded, and a great star from heaven "called Wormwood" fell into one-third "of the rivers, and upon the fountains of waters; . . . and many men died" because of the poisoned waters. The fourth angel sounded, and the third part of the sun, moon, and stars were darkened, and the light of the night and day were darkened by one-third. This was a curse on the heavens and the atmosphere. It is possible that here is meant that the day and night will be shortened by one-third to leave a sixteen-hour day. This would fulfill the Tribulation passage prophecy of Matthew 24:22: "And except those days should be shortened, there should no flesh be saved: but for the elect's sake those days shall be shortened."

In verse 13 another angel flew through the heavens

"saying with a loud voice, Woe, woe, woe, to the inhabiters of the earth by reason of the other voices of the trumpet of the three angels, which are yet to sound!" How could we imagine anything worse than the first four trumpets? Walvoord says that the first four trumpets deal with the physical world that men take for granted. The blessing of the green grass; the beauty and benefit of the trees; both fresh water and sea water; the blessings from the sun, moon, and stars; and the handiwork of God in the stars.

In chapter nine, we find the fifth and sixth trumpets. In the sounding of the fifth trumpet we see a tremendous increase in demonic activity. In verses 1 and 2 we read:

> And the fifth angel sounded, and I saw a star fall from heaven unto the earth: and to him was given the key of the bottomless pit. And he opened the bottomless pit; and there arose a smoke out of the pit, as the smoke of a great furnace; and the sun and the air were darkened by reason of the smoke of the pit.

We see in verse 1 that the star was an angel because of the use of the pronoun "him," and also "he" in verse 2. This angel was given the key to the bottomless pit. Luke 8:31 refers to the abyss or the bottomless pit as the abode of demons. This angel is also spoken of in Revelation 20:1, as having "the key of the bottomless pit." It appears that this angel is a holy angel, and there is only one angel with the one key.

Both Walvoord and Ryrie believe the angel of 9:1 to

be one and the same with the angel of the bottomless pit of verse 11 and yet different from the angel in 20:1. Walvoord continues:

> It may be concluded that the pit of the abyss is none other than the place of detention of wicked angels. It is here that Satan himself is confined for a thousand years during the reign of Christ on earth (20:1–3). The opening verse of this chapter, therefore, presents Satan as having the key to the pit of the abyss with power to release those who are confined there.
>
> —*The Revelation of Jesus Christ,* p. 162

This seems unlikely, because the angel of 9:1 is given the key, and the angel of 20:1 already has the key because he was given it in 9:1. In 9:11 we see "the angel of the bottomless pit," not the angel with the key to the bottomless pit. His name is *Abaddon* in the Hebrew tongue, and *Apollyon* in the Greek tongue, which means "destruction." He is the king of these demons and has been incarcerated with them until this point in time.

In verse 3 we are introduced to the locusts that come out of the smoke and have the sting of a scorpion. Never has there been such a beast released upon mankind. They are commanded to not eat the grass or trees (vs. 4) that is normal fare for locusts. They evidently have the power to kill with their stings because they are commanded not to kill, but to torment for five months (vs. 5). They are described as horses prepared for battle (vs. 7), with crowns of gold and faces of men (vs. 7), with the hair of women and the teeth of lions (vs. 8), breastplates of iron and wings that sound like chariots going to battle (vs. 9), with stings in their tails with which to torment men for five months. These are locusts like this world has never seen, and are pictured as locusts because of the judgment they represent in other passages in the Bible. Walvoord states that "inasmuch as demons do not have physical shape, what John is seeing must symbolize demonic possession" (*The Revelation of Jesus Christ*, p. 162).

Diametrically opposed to the view that Revelation 9 is prophetic is Uriah Smith. He views that the entire ninth chapter was historically fulfilled by the Moslem invaders beginning from the seventh century through the nineteenth century. He believes that the star that fell was Islam, and that the "bottomless pit" could possibly be the Arabian desert. It is also noted that he describes the "smoke from the bottomless pit" as the religion of Islam. The "locusts" are described as Arabs, and their sting is their indecent actions and contemptuous words. The "seal of God" are the intelligent observers of the Sabbath, and the description of the locusts fit the profile of the Arabian horse with a savage Saracen on his back. The names of Abaddon and Apollyon are describing the Ottoman government and the "angel of the bottomless pit" is his chief minister of religion.

While we must agree that Islam is the scourge of the earth, we cannot place this scenario into Revelation 9. This chapter is in the first half of the Tribulation period, and Smith's begins in the early part of the seventh century. If this scourge began in A.D. 69, which of necessity would be during the first half of the Tribulation, then adding seven years for duration of the Tribulation and another one thousand years for the Millennium would put us into New Jerusalem for over nine hundred years. This is Russellism theology, and even they cannot explain why we still have all the natural elements remaining and are experiencing the turmoil of war with the threat of destruction.

In Revelation 9:13 we see the sounding of the sixth trumpet. This angel was instructed to loose the four angels that are bound in the Euphrates River (vs. 14). These could possibly be part of the angels that are bound, mentioned in Jude 6. Therefore, it must be concluded that they are evil angels for there is no mention of holy angels ever bound, nor a reason for them to be bound. They are bound until a specific time: an hour, a day, a month, and a year (vs. 15). At God's exact time they are released to kill a third of the remaining men.

The tool that the angels are to use to kill one-third of the men is an army of 200 million horsemen. Although the origin of these horsemen is not given, there is a similar invasion mentioned in 16:12 which also comes from the east. Some believe that these are two different entries of the same event. However, the horsemen released from the River Euphrates are most certainly demons, and the kings of the east will be leading armies of men. These demons therefore are probably the angels that left their first estate of Genesis 6, or they are demons that have been specifically reserved for this purpose only. We read on in the *Ryrie Study Bible:* "The 200,000,000 creatures who compose this supernatural cavalry may be human beings or demons or demon-possessed humans."

Unger adds:

> Whether these strange, bizarre spirit-beings, with their hideous composite constitution, and their death-dealing power, are to be classified as demonic agencies, cannot be clearly ascertained. That they are demonic agents is extremely likely. Fantastic shapes and forms of demons are among their striking characteristics in extra-Biblical conceptions.
>
> —*Biblical Demonology,* p. 71

They had "breastplates of fire, and of jacinth, and brimstone" (9:17).

Then John describes the horses that these demons sat upon. They are depicted as horses from hell as they are described as modern war machines. These mounts have the heads of lions and fire and brimstone came out of their mouths. This is descriptive of something straight out of the pits of hell. Their tails are like serpents that have heads. Evidently these serpent-like tails have the poisonous bite of a viper.

The Mighty Angel with the Little Book

The time between chapter 10:1 and 11:15 does not advance the narrative. In verse 1 we see the introduction of a "mighty angel." This angel's description is quite remarkable. "And I saw another mighty angel come down from heaven, clothed with a cloud: and a rainbow was upon his head, and his face was as it were the sun, and his feet as pillars of fire." His identity is not given; he is simply called a "mighty angel." Some writers believe that this is none other than Jesus Christ, based upon the description given here. Walvoord writes: "Though the angel is presented as one having great majesty and power, there is no clear evidence that his function or his person is more than that of a created angel to whom has been entrusted great authority" (*The Revelation of Jesus Christ,* p. 170).

Seiss disagrees with Walvoord and states that the mighty angel is the Lord Jesus. He has "the rainbow on his head"—not *a* rainbow, but *the* rainbow. He also adds that the cloud is always connected with the presence of Deity. His face shone like the sun as it did the day that He appeared to Paul on the road to Damascus. He placed His right foot upon the sea and the left foot upon the earth expressing His possession. No angel was ever pictured like unto this.

The Angel and the Two Witnesses. The angel in the eleventh chapter is most likely the same "mighty angel" of the tenth chapter. The narration of chapter ten continues into chapter eleven and the proof is given in verse 3: "And I will give power unto my two witnesses, and they shall prophesy a thousand two hundred and threescore days, clothed in sackcloth." Only Christ could give this power, and the angel says that they are "my witnesses," which could only be said of Christ. This angel gives them power to kill those who try to hurt them; power to stop the rain; power to turn water to blood; and power to cause plagues whenever and wherever they desire.

Although it is not the purpose of this book to discuss subjects other than spirit beings, it is of possible interest to the reader to know the identity of the two witnesses. This we will try to do in abbreviation. There are several proposed identities of the two witnesses. Most agree that

Elijah is one of the witnesses because of the prophecy of Malachi 4:5: "Behold, I will send you Elijah the prophet before the coming of the great and dreadful day of the LORD." Even today, Jews set a chair and place setting for Elijah at the table every Passover. They believe Elijah will come on Passover to set them free and on the path to the promised Sabbath Rest. Also, each Sabbath day, the Jews expect Elijah to come. At the end of each Sabbath, when he fails to come, they light a special candle, say a prayer, sing a song, and go out. So, that only leaves the mystery as to the identity of the other witness.

These witnesses were first referred to in Zechariah 4:14: "These are the two anointed ones, that stand by the Lord of the whole earth." Here in this passage they are referred to as "two olive trees" which represent the offices of king and priest, Zerubbabel and Joshua. In Revelation 11:4, "These are the two olive trees, and the two candlesticks standing before the God of the earth," in reference to Zechariah 4:14.

Some believe the other witness to be the Church. However, the Church has already been removed at the Rapture. Some vehemently believe that he is Enoch. However, that would violate Hebrews 11:5: "By faith Enoch was translated that he should not see death." Others believe that Daniel is the other witness. After all, he was a Jew and a prophet and that seems to be a qualifying factor. However, he does not completely fill the bill.

The only other person that fulfills all the qualifications is Moses. We find the key to this precedent in Malachi 4. Here he is given a position of prominence alongside of Elijah as one of God's two witnesses, the

Law and the Prophets. Some would argue that Moses cannot represent one of the witnesses because he has experienced death as told in Deuteronomy 34:6. And Hebrews 9:27 does state, "it is appointed unto men once to die," and therefore he would seem to be disqualified. However, Jesus sets another precedence with the raising of Lazarus from the dead in John 11 that allowed him to die twice. Moses could die twice if it pleases the Lord.

Moses was a Jew of the tribe of Levi (Exod. 2:1) and a prophet (Dan. 11:17). He performed miracles during the Exodus and stated in Deuteronomy 18:15 that he still had a future work: "The LORD thy God will raise up unto thee a Prophet from the midst of thee, of thy brethren, like unto me; unto him ye shall hearken."

However, the most powerful argument is found in the Gospels. In Matthew 17:1–5, Moses appeared with Elijah at the Transfiguration of Jesus. Peter immediately recognized these two men as Moses and Elijah. How? He had never seen them before. But, he knew specifically that only these two persons could usher in the Kingdom of Heaven, a fulfillment of the Feast of Tabernacles. And if the Jews had accepted Jesus as their Messiah, this prophecy would have been fulfilled and the Millennium would have begun. Because of this, Peter immediately asked the Lord if he could build three tabernacles in observance of this event. He knew the identity of the two witnesses to be Elijah and Moses because he knew the Scriptures. Thence, we can only conclude that Elijah and Moses are the two witnesses of Revelation 11.

When Christ allows them to die, they will lie in the streets for three and one-half days before they are brought to life and ascend into heaven.

The seventh angel sounds in 11:15, and "great voices in heaven" announce: "The kingdoms of this world are become the kingdoms of our Lord, and of his Christ; and he shall reign for ever and ever." "The announcement evokes praise from the *elders* (vv. 16–17) and anger from the *nations;* and soon will come judgment on the *dead* and the rewarding of the *saints*" (*Ryrie Study Bible,* p. 1934). This teaches that it is time for divine wrath, the resurrection of the dead and their reward, and special judgment of those remaining on earth.

The Great Red Dragon. In chapter twelve we come to the midpoint of the Tribulation period, or the beginning of the "great tribulation." Satan is cast out of heaven and now becomes the center of angelic activity. Because of the judgment mentioned in chapter eleven, Satan is angry and knows his time is short. He therefore begins his onslaught against Israel and tries to destroy her and her son, Jesus Christ. There are those that say the "woman" is the Church, Christ, or even Mary, the mother of Jesus. However, the woman is Israel, the wife of Jehovah. This is easily seen in Genesis 37:9–11:

> And he dreamed yet another dream, and told it his brethren, and said, Behold, I have dreamed a dream more; and, behold, the sun and the moon and the eleven stars made obeisance to me. And he told it to his father, and to his brethren: and his father rebuked him, and said unto him, What is this dream that thou hast dreamed? Shall I and thy mother and thy brethren indeed come to bow down ourselves to thee to

> the earth? And his brethren envied him; but his father observed the saying.

Many Bible students believe that the heavenly bodies represent Jacob and Rachel, and identify the woman with the fulfillment of the Abrahamic covenant. The stars would then represent the twelve patriarchs, the sons of Jacob; the twelve tribes. The persecution of the woman parallels the persecution of Israel.

In verse 3 we are introduced to Satan. He is called a "great red dragon, having seven heads and ten horns, and seven crowns upon his heads." It is said that "his tail drew the third part of the stars of heaven" (vs. 4). As previously stated, these stars represent one-third of the angels. He has called them together to do battle against Christ and the nation of Israel to destroy them.

We once again see the providential hand of God as stated in verse 6: "And the woman fled into the wilderness, where she hath a place prepared of God, that *they* should feed her there a thousand two hundred and threescore days." The "they" can only be the "holy angels." It certainly will not be the inhabitants of the area or Satan and his forces. Today the area of Petra is unknowingly being prepared for the Jews. Since 1997 Jordan has completed a new four-lane highway from Amman through the modern city of Petra to Eilat in southern Israel. It will be very handy for the Jews to escape to Petra. Also, all new utilities have now been completed, including a new sewer system, water system, and power system. And they already have built over sixty-five hotels there in the last few years. Truly, everything will be ready for the Jews to move in, and the angels will provide the food. We also know that Jordan will be spared during the Tribulation. It shall escape the wrath of the Antichrist to be available as prophesied in Daniel 11:41: "He shall enter also into the glorious land, and many countries shall be overthrown: but these shall escape out of his hand, even Edom, and Moab, and the chief of the children of Ammon." Why would God supernaturally protect modern Jordan and the land of Edom, Moab, and Ammon? Because it is the chosen place that He will protect and provide for the Jews as they flee the presence and wrath of the Antichrist in Israel. Jordan could well be the only country that never comes under the control of Antichrist.

In Revelation 13:7 we read: "And there was war in heaven: Michael and his angels fought against the dragon; and the dragon fought and his angels." This period of time at the midpoint involves the created angels, holy and unholy. Michael as an archangel leads all the angels that are loyal to him against Satan and all of his angels. If one-third of the angels are loyal to Michael, then at least two-thirds of all the created angels will be involved in this war. It will make the Battle of Armageddon pale in comparison. This, of course, assumes that the other one-third remain on duty around the throne, having Gabriel as their leader.

In verse 9 we read: "And the great dragon was cast out, that old serpent, called the Devil, and Satan, which deceiveth the whole world: he was cast out into the earth, and his angels were cast out with him."

Now Satan is angry because he will never again be able to approach the presence of the throne of God to accuse the saints (vs. 12). The inhabitants of the heavens are told to rejoice, but the inhabitants of the earth are warned because of his great wrath. Immediately he begins to persecute Israel:

> And when the dragon saw that he was cast unto the earth, he persecuted the woman which brought forth the man child. And to the woman were given two wings of a great eagle, that she might fly into the wilderness, into her place, where she is nourished for a time, and times, and half a time, from the face of the serpent.
>
> —Revelation 12:13–14

> These two verses again describe the flight of Israel to a place of safety as the Abomination of Desolation takes place. Yet, the woman with child still pains to be delivered. This scene is described [in Isa. 26:17–18]. During the last half of the Tribulation, the time of Jacob's trouble, a remnant of Israel will hide for forty-two months until the Lord comes to bring peace out of war, order out of chaos [Rev. 12:15–17]. It seems apparent that John here was attempting to give us a clue that the hiding place of Israel would be Petra.
>
> —Noah Hutchings, *Petra in History and Prophecy,* p. 136

Satan knows now that his time is short and takes his anger out on Israel. In verse 15 John speaks of a flood being cast out of Satan's mouth. There are at least two possible explanations of this flood. First, the literal interpretation that this is a literal flood and that the earth would be able to naturally or supernaturally swallow it up. Second, the spiritual interpretation that this simply means that Satan will pull out all of the stops to destroy Israel. The dispensationalists always take the literal interpretation unless it violates other texts or is plainly meant to be spiritualized. Either way, God will intervene in Israel's behalf and usher them into their safe haven. When Satan fails with the flood, he turns his wrath on the remaining inhabitants of Jerusalem that have not accepted the mark of the Beast.

Upon returning to Jerusalem he will take his place in the Temple as prophesied in Daniel 9:27.

> And he shall confirm the covenant with many for one week: and in the midst of the week he shall cause the sacrifice and the oblation to cease, and for the overspreading of abominations he shall make it desolate, even until the consummation, and that determined shall be poured upon the desolate.

Satan, through the Antichrist, will orchestrate a seven-year peace treaty that will give the world a sense of false security. In the middle of this seven years, Satan will be cast out of heaven and begin to persecute Israel and pollute the Temple. He will then break the covenant he has made with the Jewish people and demand that the world worship him. Many believe that part of the abomination will be the offering of a sow on the altar, much the same way that Antiochus Epiphanes did as retribution against the Jews during Syria's war with Egypt in 168 B.C. Satan, the son of perdition, will enter the Temple in Jerusalem, commit the Abomination of Desolation, and sit down proclaiming himself to be God.

> Let no man deceive you by any means: for that day shall not come, except there come a falling away first, and that man of sin be revealed, the son of perdition; Who opposeth and exalteth himself above all that is called God, or that is worshipped; so that he as God sitteth in the temple of God, shewing himself that he is God.
>
> —2 Thessalonians 2:3–4

In chapter thirteen we see that Satan remains the main character, and that he is the angel that is very active continuing to empower the forces of the enemies of Christ. In verse 2 we see the rise of the Antichrist (or beast), and Satan will empower him. In verse 3 one of his heads is "wounded to death," and he is then apparently healed by Satan. However, does Satan have power of resurrection?

Dwight Pentecost doesn't think so, and in *Things to Come* he gives five reasons why the head that received a deadly wound cannot be a man. First, the reference to the healing seems to be a resurgence of the Gentile kingdom that has long been dead. Second, Satan is called the angel of the bottomless pit, or abyss, in Revelation 9:11, and Revelation 17:8 does not teach that the head came out of the abyss, rather that the empire itself was brought about from the abyss of Satan. Third, Scriptures teach that men are brought out of the grave by the voice of

God, and Satan does not have the power of resurrection. Fourth, the wicked are not resurrected until the Great White Throne. Fifth, since all the references present this individual as a man, not a supernatural being, it would seem impossible to hold him to be a resurrected individual. Walvoord agrees with Pentecost that the head that is healed is the revival of the Roman Empire.

Ryrie takes the literal approach and states in the *Ryrie Study Bible* that he believes that the head that is healed is none other than Antichrist, "wounded to death"; literally, had been slain. The same word is used in Revelation 5:6 of Christ's actual death, though here it may indicate a wound that normally would be fatal ("his deadly wound was healed"). Apparently Satan will miraculously restore Antichrist to life in imitation of the resurrection of Christ. No wonder the world will acclaim Antichrist their ruler. Ryrie has a good point in that the world will worship him, not for his political prowess, but his miracles. It might also be pointed out the possibility that a clone implant takes the place of the one wounded to death, and then appears to be the same person, carrying on as normal. Whatever the explanation, we must remember that God is using Satan and the world to bring this age to a close, and He can give an individual or Satan the power necessary to accomplish this, even the power of resurrection.

In verse 11 we see the emergence of another beast. He also speaks as a dragon and exercises the same power of the first beast, whose deadly wound was healed. This person is the false prophet. He also is empowered by Satan and makes the world to bow down to the Antichrist. He performs miracles as stated in verse 14:

> And deceiveth them that dwell on the earth by the means of those miracles which he had power to do in the sight of the beast; saying to them that dwell on the earth, that they should make an image to the beast, which had the wound by a sword, and did live.

He enforced the mandate that any that did not worship the image of the Antichrist would be killed. Then under his instruction, that the world should receive the mark of the beast, 666.

Angels of Judgment. In the fourteenth chapter the holy angels once again become the center of attention. In verse 6 an angel flies through the "midst of heaven," leading to verse 7: "Saying with a loud voice, Fear God, and give glory to him; for the hour of his judgment is come: and worship him that made heaven, and earth, and the sea, and the fountains of waters."

The message of this angel is in contrast to the message of the false prophet that the world has been forced to accept. His message is a warning that the end is near and judgment is coming. Fear God who can destroy both body and soul; not him that can destroy only the body.

In verse 8 we see a second angel that is announcing that Babylon has been destroyed. Walvoord believes this to represent the judgment of the nations, while Ryrie rather believes this to be referring to the religious center of Rome. As far as our study is concerned, this message was delivered by an angel.

In the ninth verse the third angel delivers the message to those who have accepted the mark of the beast. In verse 10 we read:

> The same shall drink of the wine of the wrath of God, which is poured out without mixture into the cup of his indignation; and he shall be tormented with fire and brimstone in the presence of the holy angels, and in the presence of the Lamb.

This will be the beginning of their torment and it shall be everlasting, "for ever and ever." The wicked will be tormented for eternity without hope of ever being released, or even annihilated.

In verse 15 another angel came out of the Temple speaking to Christ that it is time to thrust in the sickle and reap, "for the harvest of the earth is ripe." And yet another angel came out of the Temple with a sharp sickle. Then another angel came out from the altar which is said to have power over fire, and also cries for Christ to thrust in the sickle. It is then said that the angel thrust in the sickle, gathered the vine of the earth, and that blood from the winepress rose to the height of the bridle of the horses. This no doubt refers to the battle of Armageddon where the blood of the horses and men could easily rise to that level (Rev. 19:17–19).

Angels of the Seven Vials. In Revelation 16:1–21 we read of the last of the judgments, and again each one is introduced by an angel. These seem to occur in trip-hammer fashion on a world already reeling from the previous judgments. In verse 1, the angels are told to "go your ways, and pour out the vials of the wrath of God upon the earth." The first angel poured out his vial (vs. 2) and a fearful cancerous sore appeared on all that had received the mark of the beast.

The second angel (vs. 3) poured out his vial upon the sea and it became as the blood of a dead man, and every living thing in it died. The third angel poured out his vial (vs. 4) and the rivers and fountains of water became blood. The *Ryrie Study Bible* states that drinking bloody salt water would be toxic, but drinking bloody fresh water, although disgusting, would not be toxic.

The fourth angel poured out his vial (vs. 8) upon the sun and it became much hotter and scorched the backs of men. This plague seems to only affect those who have received the mark of the beast, because those affected blasphemed the name of God. It might be like the furnace that was heated seven times hotter to kill the three Hebrew children in Daniel 3:19. While God protected his men, those that belonged to Nebuchadnezzar were burned up (vs. 22). The fifth angel poured out his vial (vs. 10) upon the seat of the beast and turned his kingdom into total darkness. Those that have experienced total darkness, such as being deep in some cavern, know that the total absence of light completely disorients a person. You have no sense of direction and are in complete disarray, uncertain of your nearness to a precipice.

The sixth angel poured out his vial (vs. 12) upon the Euphrates River and caused it to dry up. This will be done to allow the kings of the east and their vast armies to cross over on dry ground. Some would say that this is possible because of the great dam that has been built across the river. However, this seems to be a supernatural act that requires the action of God's angel. This is a small thing compared to drying up the crossing path through the Red Sea to allow the Hebrews to cross over dry shod.

In verse 13 we read: "And I saw three unclean spirits like frogs come out of the mouth of the dragon, and out of the mouth of the beast, and out of the mouth of the false prophet." Although the frog is not actually mentioned in the levitical law as unclean, it was one of the unclean plagues of Egypt in Exodus 8. The Jews classified the frog unclean, believing it to be one of the unclean animals listed in Leviticus 11:29–30.

> In Rev. 16:13 certain foul spirits are said to look like frogs. The ancient Egyptians made the frog a symbol of life and origin, and an emblem of Heqet, the patron-goddess of birth. She is depicted with a frog's head, giving life to the newborn. Thus the deity was discredited when the power of Yahweh afflicted Egypt with the very animal that was her symbol.
>
> —*Wycliffe Bible Encyclopedia, Vol. 1,* p. 94

These spirits are out of the counterfeit trinity. They are the evil trio of Satan, the beast, and the false prophet. The dragon represents Satan, the beast is the Antichrist, and the false prophet represents the religious leader. And God gathered all the armies of the world to a place called Armageddon.

The seventh angel poured out his vial (vs. 17) into the air, "and there came a great voice out of the temple of heaven, from the throne, saying, It is done." The result of this vial was voices, thunders, lightnings, and a great earthquake; Babylon was split into three sections; the islands and mountains disappeared; and great hail the weight of a talent (approximately one hundred pounds) fell on the earth.

In chapter seventeen one of the seven angels that had the vials came to John and said, "Come hither; I will shew unto thee the judgment of the great whore that sitteth upon many waters" (vs. 1). The angel then explained to John about the kings of the earth, the great whore of Babylon, the beast, and the meaning of the seven heads and ten horns. The reference to "seven mountains, on which the woman sitteth" (vs. 9) is believed to be Rome because the city is built upon seven hills. The ten kings (vs. 12) are believed to be a ten-nation federation which is the revived Roman Empire. The waters "where the whore sitteth" (vs. 15) is believed to be the apostate or ecumenical church.

In chapter 18:2 we read of the angel's announcement that commercial Babylon "is fallen" or has been destroyed. Whereas the religious Babylon was earlier lamented as being destroyed by the commercial Babylon, the destruction of commercial Babylon is now being lamented by the kings (vs. 9) that participated in her sinful trade. In verse 21 a mighty angel picked up a stone like a great millstone and cast it into the sea, representing the final and complete destruction of the city of Babylon. In verse 5 her sins had reached into heaven, similar to the sins of the original city of Babylon. They were finally successful in reaching into heaven with their sins and it caused its destruction once again, this time forever.

In chapter nineteen the angel brings the message that the bride of Christ is now ready for the marriage supper of the Lamb. During the Tribulation the raptured saints have attended the judgment seat (Bema Seat) of 2 Corinthians 5:10, and have received their crowns according to their works—not there to be judged whether or not they are saved, but there because they are saved. The result is reward or loss of reward, "but he himself shall be saved" (1 Cor. 3:11–15).

The marriage of the Lamb to His bride, the Church, is a picture of the Jewish wedding. The bride would be promised to the groom sometimes from birth; in this case from the rebirth. When the time came the groom would go to the house of the bride's parents and claim her. However, before he could consummate the marriage, he had to go and prepare their home. When the home was prepared, the bridegroom would return and claim (redeem) his bride. She would place her dowry at his feet and they would then attend a marriage supper prepared for their wedding. This is the message of John 14:1–4.

> Let not your heart be troubled: ye believe in God, believe also in me. In my Father's house are many mansions: if it were not so, I would have told you. I go to prepare a place for you. And if I go and prepare a place for you, I will come again, and receive you unto myself; that where I am, there ye may be also. And whither I go ye know, and the way ye know.

In verse 17 the angel invites all the fowls of the air that eat carrion to join in a great feast of those who are about to die. Then the beast and the false prophet are cast alive into the lake of fire, never to be brought out again, not even at the Great White Throne Judgment. Then, the remaining armies of Satan are killed by Christ, and the fowls gorge themselves on their flesh. In Isaiah 34:1–3, 8, 15, we read:

> Come near, ye nations, to hear. . . . For the indignation of the LORD is upon all nations, and his fury upon all their armies. . . . Their slain also shall be cast out, and their stink shall come up out of their carcases. . . . For it is the day of the LORD's vengeance, and the year of recompences for the controversy of Zion. . . . There shall the vultures also be gathered, every one with her mate.

The vultures have been on the decline in Israel for many centuries. However, that seems to be changing. Dr. Noah Hutchings brings us up to date on the state of the vultures.

> However, for the first time in centuries, vultures are again nesting in Israel. The Israeli air force avoids vulture nesting areas during the mating and hatching seasons. Reports have indicated that vultures in Israel are laying two eggs now instead of the usual one egg; but such reports are in error. Vultures in Gamla are now laying four eggs at one nesting. This is circumstantial evidence that God is increasing the bird population of Israel for the coming Battle of Armageddon.
>
> —*Why I Still Believe These Are the Last Days,* p. 13

While recently visiting Gamla in Israel, we witnessed first-hand the unusual number of these birds. This completes the battle to reclaim the earth and bring it under the maintenance and supervision of the Lord. Now we will enter another dispensation.

Chapter Eight

The Ministry of Angels During the Millennial Dispensation of the Kingdom

The close of the Tribulation period will also bring to a close the seventieth week of Daniel. With its passing we enter the last of the dispensations, the Millennium or the kingdom of heaven. In this one-thousand–year period, Christ will repossess the earth and will reign as King. This period opens with the binding of Satan and casting him into the bottomless pit. In this period righteousness will prevail and offenders will be dealt with swiftly and firmly by Christ, who will rule with a "rod of iron." It will end with the release of Satan and the gathering of those that would rebel with him. These will bind together in a final attempt to overthrow Christ. They will fail and be destroyed by fire from heaven. This is called the battle of "Gog and Magog."

This dispensation opens in Revelation 20 with the

binding of Satan. In verse 1 we read of an angel that has the key to the bottomless pit taking a chain and binding Satan (vs. 2) and casting him into "the bottomless pit" (vs. 3). In verse 3 we read:

> And cast him into the bottomless pit, and shut him up, and set a seal upon him, that he should deceive the nations no more, till the thousand years should be fulfilled: and after that he must be loosed a little season.

He is not only chained, but he is also shut up and the door is locked. There is no possibility of escape. Satan is an angel and therefore a spirit, so no physical cage can hold him. Therefore, the bottomless pit is a place that is especially formed for the spirit world.

Satan will be removed and bound for a thousand years, but what about his demons? Will they still be free to roam the earth and cause havoc? We read what we believe to be the answer to this in Isaiah 24:21–23:

> And it shall come to pass in that day, that the LORD shall punish the host of the high ones that are on high, and the kings of the earth upon the earth. And they shall be gathered together, as prisoners are gathered in the pit, and shall be shut up in the prison, and after many days shall they be visited. Then the moon shall be confounded, and the sun ashamed, when the LORD of hosts shall reign in mount Zion, and in Jerusalem, and before his ancients gloriously.

This is a physical description of the end of the Tribulation and the beginning of the thousand-year reign. These demons will be shut up in the same pit in which Satan will be chained, and remain there until released for "a little season" prior to the battle of Gog and Magog.

With the removal of the demonic (as well as satanic) activity there is little holy angelic activity mentioned during this thousand-year period. Since there is no activity, we will not dwell on something the Bible doesn't mention. However, we might mention the conditions during the Millennium found in the book of Isaiah. There will be peace (2:4); joy (9:3-4); holiness (1:26–27); glory (24:23); comfort (12:1–2); justice (9:7); full knowledge (11:1–2); instruction (2:2–3); removal of the curse (11:6–9); removal of sickness (33:24); healing of the deformed (29:17–19); protection (41:8–14); freedom from oppression (14:3–6); no immaturity (65:20); labor (62:8–9); economic prosperity (4:1); increase of light (4:5); the fullness of the Spirit (32:13–15); and unified worship (45:23). Other conditions include the manifest presence of God (Ezek. 37:27–28); reproduction by the living peoples (Jer. 30:20); unified language (Zeph. 3:9); and the perpetuity of the millennium state (Joel 3:20).

The last we read of satanic or demonic activity is after the thousand years are completed (Rev. 20:7–8). When Satan is released out of his prison we assume that his demons are also released at the same time as their leader, because Isaiah 24 states that they will be "visited after many days." They will gather the forces of peoples that are numbered as the sand of the sea. These are the nations that lived through the thousand-year period and bowed only the knee, never the heart. They, with the devil, will be "cast into the lake of fire and brimstone, where the beast and the false prophet are, and shall be tormented day and night for ever and ever" (Rev. 20:10). The beast and the false prophet are the first by one thousand years to be cast into "the lake of fire." After this point we shall never see or hear from Satan and his forces again.

In verse 11, the Great White Throne Judgment takes place and the unsaved and ungodly will be forever cast into "the lake of fire," where the beast, false prophet, and Satan are already confined.

The record of the ministry of angels closes with the angel that brought John this great vision. When John heard the words of Christ in Revelation 22:7, he fell at the feet of the angel to worship him for the words of comfort that he had brought. The final words of the angel are found in Revelation 22:9, "Then saith he unto me, See thou do it not: for I am thy fellowservant, and of thy brethren the prophets, and of them which keep the sayings of this book: worship God."

Conclusion

The biblical study of angels is not an easy study, but it is a rewarding study. It produces a correct understanding and belief of exactly what the Bible says about them, not what the world would have us to believe. Angels have been and will continue to be active in every dispensation until the consummation of the ages.

We have found that the angels were created before the foundation of the world. They were present when the Lord explained to them how it was to be formed. Soon after they were created, one-third of them followed Lucifer when he fell because of pride. They were present at the creation of every living thing and watched with pride as God breathed the breath of life into every living thing.

They were present in the garden of Eden as the serpent deceived Adam and Eve and caused the fall of mankind, thereby bringing about the need of a Savior.

They witnessed the building of the ark and watched as Noah and his family along with some of every animal followed them in to preserve every species. Some were busy cohabiting with the daughters of men and thereby were imprisoned until the end of time. They were messengers taking messages back and forth between God and man, some between Satan and man.

They watched as man failed in his ability to govern himself and made the Law necessary. They accompanied Israel through the desert and escorted them into the Promised Land. They were always there to insure their victory until they strayed away from God.

They attended every prophet in his quest to warn Israel away from idolatry. They were there in the form of Satan's emissaries to try to foil the work of God at every turn. Angels witnessed every hardship and victory of the Old Testament saints. They were the silent partners that protected and comforted the great men of God.

The angels announced the birth of Christ and attended to His every need, although some, called demons, constantly contrived to defeat Christ and his angels. They were His constant companions as He withstood every possible physical, mental, and spiritual hardship that could come upon man. They were standing by and ready to deliver Him from the cross if they were allowed. The angels were there to roll back the stone to show the believers that He had risen. When He ascended into heaven, it was an angel that stood by to announce to the world that He would return.

During the age of grace, they stand by awaiting the Lord to command them to intervene in the lives of the saints, for they are ministering spirits—perhaps every one assigned to a different person. There is rejoicing in their presence when a person receives the Son of God, the One that they worship and adore. We have evidence in Luke, with the death of Lazarus, that they await the death of the saints and escort them into the presence of the Lord.

They will attend Jesus when He comes back to remove His saints at the Rapture. Angels will be present in heaven during the Bema Seat longing to be part of the bride and wanting to look into this thing called salvation.

The angels, both holy and fallen, will play a vital role in the Tribulation period. They were the messengers of God that delivered to John the vision of the Revelation of Jesus Christ. They will open the seals, blow the trumpets, and pour out the seven vials. The demons will also have their part in supporting Satan, as well as carrying out their own demonic activities.

When the Tribulation is over, the demons along with Satan will be cast into the "bottomless pit," while the holy angels will attend the saints and the King in His administration of the Millennium. The holy angels are forever, ageless, tireless, and will, along with the saints, experience the vastness of eternity with the Lord Jesus Christ. The most important message that comes from this study is to convey that God has provided a way to escape His judgment. It is called the plan of salvation.

God's Plan of Salvation

Why do we need to be saved? Because we have sinned against God.

In Genesis chapters one through three, we read of the creation of Adam and Eve. In chapter two, verse 7, we read about the creation of Adam:

> And the LORD God formed man of the dust of the ground, and breathed into his nostrils the breath of life; and man became a living soul.

In chapter two, verses 21 and 22, we read of the beginning of Eve's life:

> And the LORD God caused a deep sleep to fall upon Adam, and he slept: and he took one of his ribs, and closed up the flesh instead thereof; And the rib, which the LORD God had taken from man, made he a woman, and brought her unto the man.

They both were created perfect and God was well pleased with them as we read in Genesis 1:31:

> And God saw every thing that he had made, and, behold, it was very good.

Adam and Eve were perfect in every way except for experience in making decisions about right and wrong. We read the story about their sin in Genesis chapter three. They were placed into the garden of Eden and their only restriction was that they could not eat of the "tree of the knowledge of good and evil." Other than that restriction they could eat of every other vegetable and fruit. Soon after they were created, Satan approached them disguised as a serpent. The serpent told them that if they ate of the fruit of the "tree of the knowledge of good and evil" that their eyes would be opened and they would "be as gods." Adam and Eve both ate of the fruit. As a result, they both were cursed. Their sin or curse is now an inherited trait that is within every person when they are born. Their sin not only caused spiritual separation and loss of fellowship with their Creator, it also caused eventual physical death. Therefore, a Savior had to be provided to restore fellowship with God. This Savior was promised in Genesis 3:15.

Who is the Savior that can restore fellowship with God? Jesus.

> And all things are of God, who hath reconciled us to himself by *Jesus Christ*, and hath given to us the ministry of reconciliation.
>
> —2 Corinthians 5:18

> Neither is there salvation in any other [Jesus Christ]: for there is none other name under heaven given among men, whereby we must be saved.
>
> —Acts 4:12

> But God commendeth his love toward us, in that, while we were yet sinners, Christ died for us. Much more then, being now justified by his blood, we shall be saved from wrath through him. For if, when we were enemies, we were reconciled to God by the death of his Son, much more, being reconciled, we shall be saved by his life.
>
> —Romans 5:8–10

Who needs to be saved? Everyone.

Everyone is a sinner and must be saved. Adam's sin was passed upon *all* men as presented in Romans 5:12:

> Wherefore, as by one man [Adam] sin entered into the world, and death by sin; and so death passed upon *all* men, for that *all* have sinned.

Therefore everyone must be saved:

> For *all* have sinned, and come short of the glory of God.
>
> —Romans 3:23

> . . . There is none righteous, no, not one.
>
> —Roman 3:10

Who can be saved? Everyone.

> For God so loved the world, that he gave his only begotten Son, that *whosoever* believeth in him should not perish, but have everlasting life.
>
> —John 3:16

> The Lord is not slack concerning his promise, as some men count slackness; but is longsuffering to us-ward, not willing that any should perish, but that all should come to repentance.
>
> —2 Peter 3:9

> Who [Jesus] will have all men to be saved, and to come unto the knowledge of the truth.
>
> —1 Timothy 2:4

How can we be saved? Through faith in Jesus Christ, not good deeds.

> For by grace are ye saved through faith; and that not of yourselves: it is the gift of God: Not of works, lest any man should boast.
>
> —Ephesians 2:8–9

What must you do to be saved? Pray, and ask God to forgive you of your sins and receive Him as Savior according to Scripture.

> That if thou shalt confess with thy mouth the Lord Jesus, and shalt believe in thine heart that God hath raised him from the dead, thou shalt be saved. For with the heart man believeth unto righteousness; and with the mouth confession is made unto salvation. . . . For whosoever shall call upon the name of the Lord shall be saved. . . . So then faith cometh by hearing, and hearing by the Word of God.
>
> —Romans 10:9–10, 13, 17

How can you then know that you are saved?

> He that believeth on the Son of God hath the witness in himself: he that believeth not God hath made him a liar; because he believeth not the record that God gave his Son. And this is the record, that God hath given to us eternal life, and this life is in his Son. He that hath the Son hath life; and he that hath not the Son of God hath not life. These things have I written unto you that believe on the name of the Son of God; that ye may know that ye have eternal life, and that ye may believe on the name of the Son of God.
>
> —1 John 5:10–13

Our prayer is that you will accept Jesus Christ as your personal Savior and become a faithful and active member of a local New Testament church that uses the Bible for its only rule of faith and practice.

Bibliography

The Book of Enoch. Muskogee: Artisan Sales, 1980.

Brown, D. A. *Commentary, Vol. 3.* Grand Rapids, Eerdmans.

Bullinger, E. W. *Commentary on Revelation.* Grand Rapids: Kregel, 1984.

Chafer, Lewis Sperry. *Systematic Theology, Vol. 5.* Grand Rapids: Kregel, Vol. 5, 1993.

Chafer, Lewis Sperry. *Major Bible Themes.* Grand Rapids: Zondervan, 1974.

Delitzsch, F. *Commentary on the Old Testament, Vol. 1.* Grand Rapids: Eerdmans.

Dickason, Fred C. *Names of Angels.* Chicago: Moody Press, 1997.

Edershiem, Alfred. *Bible History, Old Testament.* Peabody: Hendrickson.

Fausset, A. R. *A Commentary on the Old Testament, Vol. 2.* Grand Rapids: Eerdmans.

Gaebelein, A. C. *The Angels of God.* Grand Rapids: Baker.

Gibbon, Edward. *The History of The Decline and Fall of the Roman Empire, Vol. 2.* Bigelow and Brown: New York, Chapter 15.

Haldeman, I. M. *The Tabernacle Priesthood and Offerings.* New York: Revell, 1925.

Hauser, Charles. Denver Baptist Theological Seminary. Unpublished Notes, 1976.

Henry, Matthew. *Commentary on the Whole Bible, Vol. 6.*

Hill, Edward. *Believing Bible Study.* Des Moines: The Christian Research Press, 1977.

Hodge, Charles. *Systematic Theology, Vol. 1.* Grand Rapids: Eerdmans.

Hutchings, N. W. *Petra in History and Prophecy.* Oklahoma City: Hearthstone, 1991.

Hutchings, N. W. *Why I Still Believe These are the Last Days.* Oklahoma City: Hearthstone, 1993.

Hutchings, N. W. *Why So Many Churches?* Hearthstone: Oklahoma City, 1992.

Jamison, Robert. *A Commentary, Vol. 1.* Grand Rapids: Eerdmans.
Josephus, Flavius. *Antiquities of the Jews.* Grand Rapids: Baker, 1974.
Keil, C. F. *Commentary on the Old Testament, Vol. 1.* Grand Rapids: Eerdmans.
Larkin, Clarence. *The Book of Revelation.* Philadelphia: Rev. Clarence Larkin Estate, 1919.
Moorehead, W. G. *The Tabernacle.* Grand Rapids: Kregel, 1957.
Morgan, G. Campbell. *Studies in the Four Gospels.* Old Tappan: Revell, 1931.
Pentecost, J. Dwight. *Things to Come.* Grand Rapids: Zondervon, 1958.
Philo. *The Works of Philo.* Peabody: Hendrickson, 1993.
Pictorial Encyclopedia of the Bible. Grand Rapids, Zondervan, 1976.
Rhodes, Ron. *The Complete Book of Bible Answers.* Harvest House: Eugene, 1997.
Ridout, S. *Lectures on the Tabernacle.* New York: Loizeaux Brothers.
Ryrie, Charles. *Basic Theology.* Colorado Springs: Chariot Victor, 1981.
Ryrie, Charles. *Dispensationalism.* Chicago: Moody Press, 1995.
Ryrie, Charles. *Ryrie Study Bible.* Chicago: Moody Press, 1994.
The Scofield Reference Bible. New York: Oxford, 1917.
Seiss, Joseph. *The Apocalypse.* Grand Rapids: Kregel, 1987.
Smith, Uriah. *Daniel and the Revelation.* Nashville: Southern Publishing Association, 1944.
Smith's Bible Dictionary. Iowa Falls: Riverside, 1979.
Strauss, Lehman. *The Prophecies of Daniel.* Neptune: Loizeaux Brothers, 1969.
Strong's Exhaustive Concordance. Grand Rapids: Associated Authors
Textus Receptus. Brampton: Trinitarian Bible Society. 1994.
Thiessen, Henry. *Lectures in Systematic Theology.* Grand Rapids: Eerdmans, 1979.
Unger, Merrill E. *Biblical Demonology.* Wheaton: Scripture Press, 1952.
Vincent, Marvin R. *Word Studies in the New Testament, Vol. 3.* Peabody: Hendrickson.
Walvoord, John. *Matthew, Thy Kingdom Come.* Chicago: Moody, 1974.
Walvoord, John F. *The Revelation of Jesus Christ.* Chicago: Moody, 1966.
Willmington, Harold. *Bible Handbook.* Wheaton: Tyndale House, 1997.
Wuest, Kenneth. *Word Studies in the Greek New Testament, Vol. 2.* Grand Rapids: Eerdmans, 1970.
Wycliffe Bible Commentary. Chicago: Moody, 1962.
Wycliffe's Bible Encyclopedia, Vol. 2. Chicago: Moody, 1975.

About the Author

Dr. Bob Glaze was ordained to gospel ministry in April 1969. He married his wife, Peggy, in 1960. They have two children and four grandchildren. He was involved in church work in Texas and Missouri from 1969 to 1995, and in January 1996 joined the staff of Southwest Radio Church as general manager. He received his Ph.D. in Biblical Studies from Louisiana Baptist University of Shreveport in 1998. Bob is member of the Board of Trustees of Southwest Radio Church, Inc., vice-president of Hearthstone Publishing, Ltd., and co-director of Watchman Media, Inc. He is also involved in mission tours to the Middle East and China, and is a speaker for Southwest Radio Church prophecy conferences. He and his wife reside in Oklahoma City.